THE
SACRED
RIPPLE

THE
SACRED
RIPPLE

MARIAN NEWELL

CREATION
HOUSE

The Sacred Ripple by Marian Newell
Published by Creation House
A Charisma Media Company
600 Rinehart Road
Lake Mary, Florida 32746
www.charismamedia.com

Unless otherwise noted, all Scripture quotations are from the New King James Version of the Bible. Copyright © 1979, 1980, 1982 by Thomas Nelson, Inc., publishers. Used by permission.

Scripture quotations marked NIV are from the Holy Bible, New International Version of the Bible. Copyright © 1973, 1978, 1984, International Bible Society. Used by permission.

Scripture quotations marked ESV are from the Holy Bible, English Standard Version, Copyright © 2001 by Crossway Bibles, a division of Good News Publishers. Used by permission.

Scripture quotations marked KJV are from the King James Version of the Bible.

Scripture quotations marked NLT are from the Holy Bible, New Living Translation, copyright © 2007. Used by permission of Tyndale House Publishers, Inc., Wheaton, IL 60189. All rights reserved.

Scripture quotations marked MSG are from *The Message: The Bible in Contemporary English*, copyright © 1993, 1994, 1995, 1996, 2000, 2001, 2002. Used by permission of NavPress Publishing Group.

Scripture quotations marked NASB are from the New American Standard Bible®, Copyright © 1960, 1962, 1963, 1968, 1971, 1972, 1973, 1975, 1977, 1995 by The Lockman Foundation. Used by permission.

Cover design by Nathan Morgan

Copyright © 2016 by Marian Newell
All rights reserved.
Visit the author's website: thesacredripple.com
Library of Congress Control Number: 2016938857
International Standard Book Number: 978-1-62998-554-1
E-book International Standard Book Number: 978-1-62998-555-8

First edition

16 17 18 19 20 — 9 8 7 6 5 4 3 2 1

Printed in the United States of America

DEDICATION

This book is dedicated to:

God, for giving me the strength to write the story He has given me so far. I look forward to what He has next for me. May He be glorified!

*My precious son Jesse who inspired this book. He showed me not only to persevere when the road gets tough, but also to always have **HOPE**. He taught me that laughter is the best medicine. He taught me what the word **COURAGE** means by fighting his fight with such amazing resilience. I am thankful that Jesse was and still is an example for us to look toward others who are struggling so that our struggles diminish. I am grateful to him, most amazingly, for being the child who revealed to me life's true meaning....*
"In the end it's not the years in your life that count; it's the life in your years." —Abraham Lincoln

My husband Chip for his love, a true reflection of our heavenly Father's. I thank him for enabling me to be free to be the woman God created me to be and for encouraging me to write these stories. I feel so blessed to share a life with him where we can laugh together, cry together, grow together spiritually and most importantly, pray together.

Contents

FOREWORD

We fasted and prayed for Jesse's healing. We believed and obeyed the words of the Apostle James for his healing: "Is anyone among you sick? Then he must call for the elders of the church and they are to pray over him, anointing him with oil in the name of the Lord; and the prayer offered in faith will restore the one who is sick, and the Lord will raise him up, and if he has committed sins, they will be forgiven him" (James 5: 14–15, NASB). It made sense to us that God would heal this young man who was so special to all of us. When I came to New York from Atlanta to pastor the church, I felt that one of the reasons God had brought me here was to lead the fight for Jesse's healing. It felt at times as though cancer was a person we were fighting, and my role was to rally the church on Jesse's behalf.

We took our cues from Jesse as well. Jesse fought his illness. He wanted to live, and so we fought with him. Yet, the illness always seemed to be winning, and Jesse's body gave out before his spirit did. Even as he was breathing his last breaths, we had hope for resurrection. The Spirit of the Lord was manifestly present in Jesse's hospital room. However, He had come not to raise him from the dead, but to take him home, to take him from his broken body to his glorified body, to take him from this broken world to the home He had been preparing for Jesse in the place where there is no suffering or sickness, where what has been lost is restored. Jesse is healed for all eternity. He has heard from his savior, "Well done." In the midst of the tremendous grief of Jesse's passing, I will never forget those last days in his hospital and the way that Jesus made himself so manifestly present to Jesse and to each of us.

No one fought harder for Jesse than Marian. She pursued every possibility for his healing. Her love for Jesse was and is inspiring. She was tireless in her love. Obviously, you could say that her love was a mother's love for her son, but the source of her love for Jesse was not just the natural love that a mother had for her son. She had tapped into a supernatural source for that love. She had a source of love and joy in the midst of her worst days of suffering. I was not in New York when Marian met Jesus and came into a special relationship with Him, but I have personally observed her ability to receive, in the hardest times, His comfort and solace, to rely and trust in Him in her moments of doubt and fear, and to receive and do His will even when it went against her own will. Because of Jesus Marian made her story about Jesus, not about Marian. In losing a son so precious, she trusted the one who redeems her pain, not only here on earth, but also in the life to come. There is no one else that worships Jesus like Marian. It is beautiful to watch her in the presence of God giving the fullness of her love to Jesus.

One final thought, if you ever lose something precious and valuable to you, the loss is very great. However, if you find it after having lost it, that precious thing becomes even more valuable to you. There are things in this life that we lose and things that we are asked to let go of. Jesus said it this way: "Truly I say to you, there is no one who has left house or brothers or sisters or mother or father or children or farms, for My sake and for the gospel's sake, but that he will receive a hundred times as much now in the present age, houses and brothers and sisters and mothers and children and farms, along with persecutions; and in the age to come, eternal life" (Mark 10:29-30, NASB). This is Marian's story—her trust in Jesus' promise. The evidence that she shares with us that He is restoring her both now in this life and in the life to come.

—DR. MICHAEL PLUNKET

LEAD PASTOR OF RISEN KING ALLIANCE CHURCH

PREFACE

I am certain that none of this has come about by anything that I have done except to surrender my life completely to The Lord and continue to pray to be in the center of His will. I pray for Him to increase my faith, that my faith will be an example to others.

"Now faith is the substance of things hoped for, the evidence of things not seen" (Hebrews 11:1, KJV). Things hoped for? Don't we all have hope at a particular time in our lives before we sometimes lose that hope? I sure hoped, and prayed, and believed that my fourteen-year-old son Jesse would be healed from cancer. I know that I know that he was healed, maybe not in the way that I, as well as those who loved him, would have hoped.

I think the key is always having hope for more even after loss. I love how D.L. Moody put it: "Faith takes God without any *IF's*." I use to believe the lie, "*If only* I had enough faith God would not have allowed Jesse to get cancer. *If only* I was a better person…" I believed that I was not good enough in God's eyes. I asked myself, "Why did this happen?"

I can recall the day I was reading God's Word and it was the first time that a peace came over me, like an answer to my question, "Why?" It was as though God was telling me that I wouldn't fully understand why now, and suddenly, it was okay not to know the reason. For now we see only a reflection as in a mirror; then we shall see face to face. Now I know in part; then I shall know fully, even as I am fully known. (1 Corinthians 13:12, NIV).

I believe when we see Jesus He would gladly answer all of our questions, but better yet, I believe that we won't have any. We will just be in awe of His love for us, be on our faces worshiping and adoring Him!

So, *"what If"* Jesse were healed physically, what would life be like now? I would hope that I would still have been thanking God every day and never losing that dependence I had on Him. I would hope that I continued to spread the word of what He had done! All I do know is that I do thank Him every day even though my son is no longer here with me. I thank Him for the time I had, for the gift of those fourteen years, for carrying us through the storm, for bringing me into a closer relationship with Him, for showing me the good that comes out of the suffering, for redeeming my life, giving me joy again, but most of all for showing me how much He loves me. I believe by faith that He knows what is best for all of us. I believe that His grace was and is sufficient in my weakness.

I pray that as you read through these true stories you will find *hope*, that you will be encouraged, that you will receive the truth from His Word, that your faith will be renewed, that you will know that He is sufficient, and that He does restore!

ACKNOWLEDGMENTS

I am thankful to so many of you that have traveled this journey with me—some have walked closely beside me, while others I have only spoken with—each of you designed by God's divine plan. A journey surely not chosen by me, yet one I have now learned to look back on with a grateful heart. To my amazing family, now so blessedly multiplied; to my friends, both old and new. Thank you for lifting me up and speaking life into my soul.

To Matt and Sami for making me so proud to be your mom. It is a privilege and precious gift I will always treasure. I know the road has not always been easy for you both; I continue to pray for love and peace to reign in your hearts always.

To my mom and dad for their love, wisdom, support, prayers and the invaluable foundation of faith they gave me. I appreciate how fortunate a start I had.

I thank my sisters Lorraine and Fran, who are not just my blood sisters, but also my sisters in Christ and my forever-best friends, as well as my brother for all the love and support.

To the father of my children, I thank you for being a good dad and for your support in raising them.

To Kim and Rocco, for getting us through those long hospital nights with good food and laughter.

To Linda, for being the one friend I know really "gets it," that our one conversation can change the day and for always thinking of others, especially me.

To Debbie, for listening to my heart, for knowing, and letting God do the rest.

To Pastor Mike and Lisa for your anointed leadership, love, and guidance and for the Risen King church family. I couldn't have lived those three years without you.

To Denise, for being there for me especially through the initial shock and for all your efforts in fundraising for Jesse's Wish.

To Georgie, my Proverbs 31 Woman, couldn't imagine life without you, grateful I will never have to.

To Mary and Marcus for your unconditional love, treasured friendship to both Chip and I, and for being an example of what it looks like to live for Jesus.

INTRODUCTION

Where do I begin to tell the story of how great a love can be? The sweet love story that is older than the sea. I can still remember 1970, watching the film "Love Story" and listening to that beautiful song, "Where Do I Begin?" I imagined what it would be like to know a love like that. "The simple truth about the love He brings to me. Where do I start?"

I always had this fairytale view of life. In my late teens I read a lot of poetry, wrote poetry, even entered a contest to have one published. The poem was accepted for publication, although I never followed through. I was too self-absorbed and focused on getting married and having babies. My dreams did come true. Life did unfold as I had planned: married at twenty-four, gave birth to three beautiful children, had a good husband and father to our children, a beautiful home, and a close-knit extended family. So what was wrong?

I had no idea why my life seemed to have this empty place that nothing would fill. My mom was a great support for me, always an example of strength. I can remember the day of the Cuban Missile Crisis. They sent us home from school. I was so scared and upset that the high school where my sisters attended did not close. I was crying to my mom, "If we are going to die today, I want us to all be together!" I remember the fear, frustration, and confusion I felt at my mom's response, "It's all in God's hands." I did not understand how she could be so calm as she went about her ironing chore that dreadful day. As history would have it we survived that awful day and life continued as "normal." In the weeks that followed I would sit in church and look at my mom's face and know that she knew something I didn't. If only I could just get a grasp on what it was. It wasn't until I was forty-six years old that I realized it wasn't something she had that I needed, it was someone, and His name is Jesus Christ!

It was July of that same year that my perfect storybook life completely shattered with the news that my eleven-year-old son Jesse had *cancer*!

He had been jumping in and out of the pool so much I just assumed his limping was that he had hurt his leg, until a low grade fever that remained had me taking him to the doctor's office. I told the doctor about his limping, and he ordered an X-Ray. He sent us the same day for an MRI that revealed a tumor the size of a grapefruit on his hip! The next day we were on our way to NYC for a biopsy. It was confirmed…Ewing's Sarcoma, a rare bone cancer for which they had only five drugs to "trial" in one of the world's largest leading cancer hospitals. Now I knew a fear like never before. It was so surreal. I could hardly wrap my mind around what was happening. I knew I needed to be strong for my family, not show fear especially to Jesse. He was such a trooper. It's pretty amazing the resilience he showed. Not to say he was never afraid. There were many days he would get angry and lie silent with tears running down his face. There is nothing worse than seeing your children in pain and feeling helpless to know what to do to make it all stop.

The faith my mom possessed, I now desperately sought after.

I wasn't quite sure just what that would mean and if I was ready to respond. I was angry and scared—this was my son. If there was one thing in my life that felt right it was being a mother. I can still picture myself in the hospital hallway hiding behind a linen rack crying and making that conscious choice to allow God in yet asking him, "*Why?*"

One of my life's callings now is to tell as many people as I can about what the Lord has done for me and to encourage them to accept Him now and not wait until they are desperate as I was when I accepted Christ.

I look back now and see how patient the Lord was for me to answer His call. I now see His intervention throughout my life.

The following true stories are about realizations I have had and many special people that God has brought into my life to surround my family. They helped get us through not only the three years of Jesse's cancer treatment but his death and the after math. These people are the sacred ripples, each a concentric circle, all of them radiating outward, intersecting and sometimes passing through the other ripples. All made by the same center: the life of one sweet boy with a strong loving spirit who touched them all with his fight.

Yes, a sweet love story that is older than the sea!

JESSE WITH HIS BROTHER MATT AND SISTER SAMI IN FLORIDA COURTESY OF MAKE-A-WISH FOUNDATION.

MOM

I'm comforted by the words in John 14 when Jesus comforted his disciples by saying, "Do not let your hearts be troubled. You believe in God; believe also in me. My Father's house has many rooms; if that were not so, would I have told you that I am going there to prepare a place for you? And if I go and prepare a place for you, I will come back and take you to be with me that you also may be where I am. You know the way to the place where I am going" (John 14: 1–4, NIV) Then Jesus promises the Holy Spirit in verse 15: "If you love me, keep my commands. And I will ask the Father, and he will give you another advocate to help you and be with you forever—the Spirit of truth. The world cannot accept him, because it neither sees him nor knows him. But you know him, for he lives with you and will be in you" (14:15–17, NIV).

These were just words that didn't really mean much to me, after all, a spirit—that was just too intangible for me. I thank the Lord every day now for having made His Word real to me, for saving me from myself, for giving me a mom who prayed for me! If He hasn't already, God wants to reveal himself to you... no matter how much you've messed up in this life. No past or present sin is too big for our God! The understanding of His grace, mercy, and the reality that His Holy Spirit lives in me overwhelms me with joy every day! I am His child! I have the identity of Christ and the power of His Holy Spirit. He will never leave me!

I grew up in, as the old saying goes, "a white bread Italian town." I felt very loved by my parents, and I miss them so much. My mom was my strong foundation. I admired her love for the Lord. I remember her telling me that she was very sick once, in bed, so she cried out to Jesus, and He came into the room, touched her, and she was healed. I didn't believe then that He could do that. I also didn't know until after she passed away that as a young mom she suffered with anxiety attacks, and He healed her from that. She trusted Him, and it showed in her life. She took everything *with a grain of salt* as the old saying goes. She always told me I needed to learn how to cope. I obviously didn't until I found Jesus. My freshman year of high school I ventured out of my little white picket fence world to go to a Catholic high school where I experienced tough girls making fun of my school uniform as I walked to the bus stop to go home. This felt a lot worse than my brother-in-law teasing me all the time. I begged my mom to let me go to our public school before those girls beat me up. My mom loved me so much she knew I needed to find my way and gave me the freedom to do so. I went to the public high school my sophomore year. I probably would've been better off getting beat up instead of beating myself up and defiling my body with marijuana. It all started in my new school with my new friend Patty. She was so pretty and popular, and she offered me my first joint. After all, it was the sixties. Who didn't smoke pot? There were many times that I looked back on those years with regret, guilt, and shame knowing how fast time goes and how much of it I wasted. Patty is no longer with us on this earth. AIDS took her life like so many others I went to high school with. Many times I wonder why I got to survive all the messes I managed to get myself into. Why am I still here when I don't deserve to be? I know it was the prayers of my mom.

If only we would recognize that we don't take our next breath unless He ordains it. I'm so happy that I don't have to look in my rearview mirror anymore. That's exactly what the enemy would have me do. He knows exactly when and where to access our thoughts to bring about worry. I remind myself to go to prayer for my children so that I don't go to fear. I fight the enemy with God's Word just as Jesus did. Second Timothy 1:7 tells us that God did not give us a spirit of fear, but of power and of love and of sound mind. It was a real struggle for me when my older son joined the military and my daughter went to college. The enemy would tell me that I would not survive if anything happened to another one of my children. He is a liar, and when he whispers those lies we sometimes react negatively if we are not standing on God's Word. I know I was annoying and overprotective towards my children when I should have been trusting God with their lives. They have grown to become loving, compassionate adults. As they watched their brother suffer they also knew that they needed God's strength to endure that trial. I pray that they continually seek Him throughout their lives. I am so proud of who they are. When I asked my daughter if she would like to contribute any memory for the book, this is what she wrote:

> When I think about my mom, the first thing that comes to mind is her strength. After losing Jesse, her parents, and her marriage, my mom didn't lose herself. She knew she had to be strong for my oldest brother Matt and for me. I was only twelve when Jesse went home to be with the Lord. Every night for months, my mom stayed with me in Jesse's room until I fell asleep. Just having her with me in his room gave me the comfort I needed. Looking back at it now, I honestly don't think I would have survived without that support from her. She is the most selfless person I've ever known and, sure,

I'm biased, but as you read you'll see her heart for the Lord and for others. She's unapologetically herself. I have personally seen how Jesse's life has already touched so many lives, and I'm excited knowing these stories will bring hope and healing to many others.

It is so important to intercede in prayer for our children. It is a privilege we should not neglect. It may take years to see answers to our prayers, but when we surrender our lives to the Lord we can trust in His promises. There are so many scriptures that refer to the authority we have in prayer as parents. I hope you take the time to speak these over your children. It will no doubt be the best thing you could ever do for them for they are surely one of God's greatest gifts. God tells us in His Word, "And He will love you and bless you and multiply you; He will also bless the fruit of your womb..." (Deuteronomy 7:13). It is never too late to start praying.

In order to fulfill the purpose I now know God had in saving me, I need to look forward, to look heavenly, to look into His face and pray continually. He has taken all my messes; all my sorrows, past, present, and future; and He has turned my ashes into beauty!

> Therefore there is now no condemnation for those who are in Christ Jesus.
>
> —ROMANS 8:1, NIV

I believe that God's grace covers our past, and His grace empowers us and propels us for our future.

> May the LORD GIVE YOU INCREASE MORE AND MORE, YOU AND YOUR CHILDREN.
>
> —PSALM 115:14

Even the captives of the mighty shall be taken away, And the prey of the terrible be delivered; For I will contend with him who contends with you, And I will save your children.

—ISAIAH 49:25

Thus says the Lord: "Refrain your voice from weeping, And your eyes from tears; For your work shall be rewarded, says the Lord, And they shall come back from the land of the enemy. There is hope in your future, says the LORD, That *your* children shall come back to their own border.

—JEREMIAH 31:16–17

Assuredly, I say to you, whatever you bind on earth will be bound in heaven, and whatever you loose on earth will be loosed in heaven.

—MATTHEW 18:18

Train up a child in the way he should go, And when he is old he will not depart from it.

—PROVERBS 22:6

For I will pour water on him who is thirsty, And floods on the dry ground; I will pour My Spirit on your descendants, And My blessing on your offspring.

—ISAIAH 44:3

Lord,

I am so grateful for the mom you gave me. Thank you for her love for you and for giving me that strong foundation to build upon. Thank you for her example of faith in how she lived her life completely trusting in you. Thank you for revealing yourself to her. I pray for the seeds she planted in our family to fall on fertile soil that we may all be together in heaven around your banquet table as we enjoyed so many days together as a family here on earth. I thank you with all my heart for giving me children and for your hand of blessing and protection on their lives. I pray that you will help me to be the spiritual inspiration and influence on my children as my mom was for me. In the name of Jesus, Amen.

My Baby Brother

Where did the years go? I remember how I loved having him as "our new baby," even though I was only four when he arrived. It was the one my dad was waiting for, he finally got his boy! Of course he was his dad's namesake, Frank. How funny now to recall him being referred to as "Frankie boy." Now the name will carry on! I felt like I lost my "Daddy's-little-girl" status when he came along, but there was never any jealousy or competition. Our dad had enough love for both of us. He did groom only Frankie for taking over the family appliance business. My dad believed women got married and had babies; that was their role in life.

My brother had a painful first marriage and divorce, subsequently losing his two daughters to their mom who moved out of state. My sisters and I felt for him and tried to be there to support him through the pain of loss, reassuring him that the way to peace was a relationship with the Lord. We never know a person's heart and should never judge them. My brother is a loving, compassionate man who got the opportunity to be married again and now has four more beautiful children. He did open up his heart to me. He knew

I was emotionally drained after the loss of our dad, my son, and a divorce. He let me know that he was there for me. I knew he was as he stood many nights with me at Jesse's bed-side. I will always be grateful that he was there with me the night before Jesse went home to be with the Lord. I got to hear the conversation about a story in the Bible he was discussing with Pastor Mike. I remember feeling grateful that he knew what he did about the story. I knew that he had heard the good news of the gospel. I also know he had a really hard time accepting Jesse's death just forty days after our dad's. Hours after Jesse went home to heaven, my family and I were leaving the room but my brother would not leave. He could not bear to leave. I looked back seeing him there so broken. I don't feel like my brother and I have a close relationship now; although, I'm sure the love is still there. Family dynamics can change so much when our parents are no longer here. I do hope and pray that there will be a renewed relationship; that my brother and I will spend more time together. I look forward to having more of those heart-to-heart talks. I pray that he will see the love of God in my husband and me. I am certain that his beautiful wife Raquel felt the presence of God at our wedding three years ago when she responded to the invitation to accept Jesus Christ. I want to assure both my brother and Raquel that God is a good God even when He allows bad things to happen. My husband and I pray for opportunities to disciple them as we continue to pray for them. Won't you join me in praying for those you love too?

> For the word of God is alive and powerful. It is sharper than the sharpest two-edged sword, cutting between soul and spirit, between joint and marrow. It exposes our innermost thoughts and desires. Nothing in all creation is hidden from God. Everything is naked and exposed before his eyes, and he is the one to whom we are accountable.
>
> —HEBREWS 4: 12–13, NLT

If we confess our sins, he is faithful and just to forgive us our sins and to cleanse us from all unrighteousness.

—1 JOHN 1:9, ESV

Judge not, and you will not be judged; condemn not, and you will not be condemned; forgive, and you will be forgiven.

—LUKE 6:37, ESV

For all have sinned and fall short of the glory of God.

—ROMANS 3:23, NIV

For by grace you have been saved through faith. And this is not your own doing; it is the gift of God.

—EPHESIANS 2:8, ESV

Father God,

We praise you in the storms of life; we praise you in the good times too. We believe that you are good, and that you love us. You are a good God, the giver of all good gifts, and you desire that none shall perish. Your Word promises that we will join you at your banquet table in heaven, having a better family gathering that we've ever known before. We pray that by the power of your Holy Spirit you would come and heal families and gather your harvest for your kingdom. We thank you for the gift of family. We look forward to seeing our loved ones again in heaven. We pray and thank you ahead of time for those who may have not yet committed their lives to you. We pray that you make it clear how salvation is a free gift from you for all who receive it. Thank you for the forgiveness of sin. In the precious name of Jesus we pray, Amen.

MARIAN'S BROTHER FRANKIE WITH JESSE
AND HIS DOG CHAZZ.

ED AND RUTH

After my children were born I found myself searching for more meaning to my life. I had gone back to school when Sami turned three, and she could stay in the nursery on campus. I worked hard for three years studying to earn a degree and was proud of my accomplishment. I soon found a great job working with children with special needs. I felt grateful for all my blessings, especially my three wonderful children. I had a nice home; I could buy pretty much what I wanted, which gave only some short-lived gratification. I still felt like something was missing in my life. I started visiting some new churches. I grew up Catholic, went to Catholic schools, believed in God, learned a lot about religion, but it didn't really mean much to me. When my son got cancer I asked my mom, "How could God give children cancer?" She simply said to me, "Don't blame God; you need Him!" I remembered a Christian church I had visited and how I was warmly greeted there, so I went back. I listened the best I could to what Pastor Ed was saying, yet I was so distraught I could hardly focus. What I did recognize was his humility and love that came through with every word he spoke. A young woman that sat beside me touched my hand during worship and asked if I wanted to step into the lobby knowing I was struggling to keep from crying. Ruth, the pastor's wife, quickly joined us. I shared my worry for my son's health and immediately found support and comfort there. At first I felt so much guilt that what happened to Jesse was my fault; that God was punishing me for my sins. Ruth reassured me that our God is a loving God, and He doesn't work that way. A few days later I received a card from Ruth with a scripture about "the fear of the Lord." Proverbs 14:26 says, "In the fear of the LORD is strong confidence: and his children shall have a place of refuge" (KJV). I wasn't sure what that meant. Ruth explained to me that fear in that context was respect for the Lord. I certainly knew I didn't have that, and I surely had a lot to learn. I opened my heart and opened the Bible for the first time in my life. I began to read John to see who God really is, His character, His promises, how He became man for us and died on the cross so that our sins would be forgiven. Pastor Ed assured me that all I needed to do was repent for my sins, accept Jesus as my savior and trust in Him, and I would be given the gift of eternal life. I started to see events occurring in my life that had to be from God. A peace, which transcends all understanding, began to come over me. Pastor Ed and Ruth were such a blessing to our family. Ruth started a prayer chain for Jesse and our family that has never ended. The church made sure we were not only spiritually taken care of but that we had meals and child care for Sami as I was gone for long hours every day going to the hospital. I continued to grow in my spiritual walk by attending Bible classes and worshiping in that church. Pastor Ed introduced Jesse and Sami to Pastor Nick and they got involved in their youth group, which was an amazing source of strength for them. Now they were hearing God's Word too while having fun with other kids their age. Nick gave Jesse his own bright blue bass guitar. I'll never forget the look on Jesse's face when he brought it home. That Christmas Jesse wrote a card: "Dear Jesus, I will try to stop swearing and making fun of my sister for you. Happy Birthday! I pray every night for you to heal me. Love, Jesse."

I also have an index card I treasure written and signed by Jesse that he brought home from youth group: "But as for me, I will always have hope, I will praise you more and more. My mouth will tell of your righteousness, of your salvation all day long, though I know not its measure" (Psalm 71:14–15, paraphrased as on card). How precious that my children were learning how to pray!

I realized that I was beginning to have a real relationship with the Lord. I was no longer just praying to Him, I was hearing back from Him! He confirmed things from His word. I realized I needed to give Him *all* the control over what was happening in my life. Yes, my life still had that terrific burden to bear, but I knew that God would never leave me alone in it and that He loved Jesse even more than I did. I dedicated my life to Him and declared Him openly as my Lord and Savior. He gave me His Holy Spirit, which His Word tells me lives in me to give me comfort, guidance, and strength, and it did! I felt new, but it wasn't just a feeling. The Bible says we become new creations, and boy did I want and need to press the "start over" button! I learned that He chose me because He wants to use me for His glory. Use me? How can that be? Story after story in the Bible shows us how He used the most unlikely, unwilling, unequipped people because none of them were really ever unequipped using His strength instead of their own. I just wanted to be obedient to Him and get to know Him more. I began to realize that He had been with me all my life, every step of the way. I have so much to be thankful for and so much to look forward to knowing heaven is my true home where I will be with Him forever.

I can still hear Pastor Ed's comforting words he spoke at Jesse's funeral admitting that we don't always understand God's ways, that He had a different plan; what we want is not always the best. As he sat in his yard the day he heard of Jesse's passing, the Lord comforted him, reminding him that this life is not all there is. We will spend more time on the other side; this is like a dress rehearsal, a time of preparation. In God's eyes Jesse was prepared. He quoted Psalm 39:4: "Lord, remind me how brief my time on earth will be. Remind me that my days are numbered—how fleeting my life is (NLT).

What I pray for now is that more people, because of my testimony, would come to know Jesus sooner, not wait until something so horrific happens that they feel desperate. It's such a waste of time to live without the joy that knowing Him can only bring! I know I will see Jesse again.

> And we know that for those who love God all things work together for good, for those who are called according to his purpose. For those whom he foreknew he also predestined to be conformed to the image of his Son, in order that he might be the firstborn among many brothers.
>
> —ROMANS 8:28–29, ESV

It says *all* things, not some. No matter how bad life seems to get, for those of us who love Him, He is going to turn that bad into something good!

> Therefore, if anyone is in Christ, he is a new creation. The old has passed away; behold, the new has come. All this is from God, who through Christ reconciled us to himself and gave us the ministry of reconciliation; that is, in Christ God was reconciling the world to himself, not counting their trespasses against them, and entrusting to us the message of reconciliation. Therefore, we are ambassadors for Christ, God making his appeal through us. We implore you on behalf of Christ, be reconciled to God. For our sake he made him to be sin who knew no sin, so that in him we might become the righteousness of God
>
> —2 CORINTHIANS 5:17–21, ESV

Remember not the former things, nor consider the things of old. Behold, I am doing a new thing; now it springs forth, do you not perceive it? I will make a way in the wilderness and rivers in the desert.

—ISAIAH 43:18–19, ESV

Your righteousness, O God, reaches to the highest heavens. You have done such wonderful things. Who can compare with you, O God? You have allowed me to suffer much hardship, but you will restore me to life again and lift me up from the depths of the earth. You will restore me to even greater honor and comfort me once again.

—PSALM 71: 19–21, NLT

[I pray] that the God of our Lord Jesus Christ, the Father of glory, may give to you the spirit of wisdom and revelation in the knowledge of Him, the eyes of your understanding being enlightened; that you may know what is the hope of His calling, what are the riches of the glory of His inheritance in the saints, and what is the exceeding greatness of His power toward us who believe, according to the working of His mighty power.

—EPHESIANS 1:17–19

JESSE ENJOYING HIS GUITAR GIVEN TO HIM BY HIS YOUTH PASTOR NICK

MIKE AND LISA

I owe so much to my dear friends Mike and Lisa. Pastor Mike and his wife Lisa had come to pastor our church just four short months prior to Jesse's funeral. I was certain that Mike was whom the Lord was going to use to bring Jesse's healing about. After hearing all the testimonies of miracles that they had witnessed, it just cemented it for me that Jesse was going to be their next testimony of a miracle. Little did I know then that it was more for my healing that they came into our lives. The love, support, friendship, teaching, and mentoring I received from them was invaluable. They immediately immersed themselves in my family, coming over for Sunday dinner and just getting to know all of us. Pastor Mike would come during the week and just sit with Jesse in his room as he played video games on days we were not at the hospital, just praying for him and loving on him. The Wednesday nights that I could get to the church for their teachings were so amazingly powerful. I really started to learn about prayer. How important it is to pray unceasingly and never stop asking until God says, "No, not this time, not this way." There was a sweet elderly man named José who told Pastor Mike to prepare my heart, that he had received word that the time was coming that Jesse would go home to be with the Lord. Mike had been in the hospital the night before along with my brother, just talking about the stories in the Bible. I remember being surprised that my brother brought up Moses, and they were discussing it. I continue to pray for all the seeds that were planted then for my family and for all those who have not made the conscious choice yet to accept Jesus as their Lord and Savior. The next day when it became imminent that Jesse was not going to be with us much longer, Pastor Mike was called and he came right back into the city to be there with us. He later said to me, "I'm sorry I didn't come straight up to you when I walked into the room; even though Jesse had already passed I wanted to go up to him and pray for resurrection." Now that's the kind of faith I want to have! One of the many things that he said to me in the days that followed was that sometimes we need to look at our broken heart as if the brokenness is just more places for God's love to flow in. That image continues to encourage me to this day. I tell that to others who are suffering to encourage them also. After all, it's quite evident to me that whatever God allows us to go through, He then puts people into our lives that need our experience, our words of encouragement, and the comfort we have found that we desire to pass on to them.

That truth is so clear in His Word!

> Blessed be the God and Father of our Lord Jesus Christ, the Father of mercies and God of all comfort, who comforts us in all our affliction, so that we may be able to comfort those who are in any affliction, with the comfort with which we ourselves are comforted by God. For as we share abundantly in Christ's sufferings, so through Christ we share abundantly in comfort too.
>
> —2 CORINTHIANS 1:3–5, ESV

I can remember standing in Jesse's room a few days later just looking out the window at the tree I planted there for him when he was a baby. Sobbing uncontrollably with grief as I spoke with Lisa on the phone, she told me to ask God for a sign that He was there with me to comfort me and lift me up. Moments later, at least five Blue Jays flocked to that tree. It was just such an awesome site, and I knew in my heart that it was from God. From that day on every time I took a walk and was praying and needed to be reassured that He was listening to me, it seems all I had to do was look and there was another Blue Jay. Lisa also said something to me that continues to this day to give me comfort. She said to remember that just like Mary, God chose me to be Jesse's mom. They pointed out to me that it's not that I had Jesse for only fourteen years, but that I received a gift from God that I had for fourteen years!

They both continue to be used by the Lord to transform hearts and change lives by being faithful shepherds and servants and allowing the Father's love to flow through them. Mike's teachings on emotional healing, which were life-saving for me, continue to be heard around the globe. He teaches the importance of being vulnerable, broken, and surrendered so that the Potter can form us into the person He created us to be, giving God the glory by walking out the assignment He has for us. The joy of the Lord is our strength no matter what our circumstances. I will admit that my journey of grief of not having my son with me is a painful one. I have been changed by it in that I am dependent on God and ever so grateful for His blessings on my life. I am so much more aware of His love for me that is never changing, always unconditional. The Bible tells us in James 1:2 that whenever we face trials, to count it all as joy. That sounds ridiculously hard. I remember when Jesse first passed it was a relief that he was no longer suffering, but then you miss the person so much that the pain feels almost unbearable. There were many days that I was so sad that all the prayers for Jesse were not answered the way I wanted them to be. I know that joy is not the same as happiness. The Lord can put joy in our hearts no matter what our circumstances. His promises are true! In Romans 8:28 Paul tells us, "We know that in *all* things God works for the good of those who love him, who have been called according to his purpose" (NIV).

It was not in the will of God to cure Jesse physically on this earth, but he was healed! Reminding myself that he is whole and perfect now, picturing him in heaven, trusting and knowing that he is in the presence of the Lord and that I will see him again someday gets me through. Seeing what God has done to redeem my life by giving me a husband who loves me in such a way that helps me to understand our heavenly Father's love is such a blessing. We both know it is part of God's plan for us both to let people know that when you walk with Jesus, He gets such pleasure in giving His children love and good gifts. He takes us out of that pit of grief and brings joy back into our hearts to show others His love and compassion.

I can't stress enough the value of belonging to a fellowship of believers that lifts you up, prays for you, and encourages each other. Having a pastor who allows the Holy Spirit to speak through him is vital. I pray you have already found this, but if not, until you do, I urge you to listen to God's teachings at Risenkingalliance.org

> The Lord is my strength and shield. I trust him with all my heart. He helps me, and my heart is filled with joy. I burst out in songs of thanksgiving.
>
> —PSALM 28:7, NLT

> Look at the birds of the air; they do not sow or reap or store away in barns, and yet your heavenly Father feeds them. Are you not much more valuable than they?
>
> —MATTHEW 6:26, NIV

> ...But because one other person obeyed God, many will be made righteous.
>
> —ROMANS 5:19, NLT

Lord,

Thank you for our pastors and leaders of your church. Bless them who work selflessly to teach your word and empty themselves to be vessels for your Holy Spirit. I pray for your continued strength, wisdom, and discernment in their lives as they lead your people. Encourage them, protect them from the enemy, and give them your revelation to reap the harvest for your kingdom. In the name of Jesus, Amen.

LIZ

What can you say about sweet Liz? Her smile is contagious, her love for the Lord undeniable. Just as Jesus came into my heart and changed me, filling that empty place I was searching to fill, He used dear Liz to do so for Jesse. Even though it took me a few years to respond to the Lord's call on my life, Liz, the person God assigned to speak into Jesse's life about Jesus, was at the same church I had visited years prior as though waiting for us to return. Yes, there was no mistaking that blue camper van parked at our home was the same one driven by the same lady who had approached Matt and me after my first visit to Risen King. Liz had invited Matt to the youth group super Bowl Sunday party back then. I recall speaking for him saying, "Thank you but he wouldn't be interested," and to my surprise he wanted to go. I remember driving him to the house it was held at and thinking, *okay I guess I can trust these church people with my son for the afternoon.* And it was those same people, after my return to that church years later, who surrounded us with love, support, and most importantly prayer!

Although there were nine elementary schools in our district, and who knows how many possible tutors, it just had to be God's appointment that the day we found out Jesse couldn't go back to school, Liz was assigned to be his home tutor. Liz had begun to pray for us before she even met us due to the church prayer chain that Ruth had begun.

Jesse immediately liked Liz and stopped feeling bad about missing his first day at middle school. She had sent me a card with this promise: "'For I know the plans I have for you,' declares the Lord, 'plans to prosper you and not to harm you, plans to give you hope and a future'" (Jeremiah 29:11, NIV). Boy, did I hold on to that promise for my son and me. I developed such a hunger for more of His word, and as I continued to read in that chapter it became like water for my soul. "Then you will call on me and come and pray to me, and I will listen to you. You will seek me and find me when you seek me with all your heart" (Jeremiah 29:12–13, NIV). I could not resist that promise, and oh how through praying and seeking Him, He so listened to my heart!

I can still see the excitement on Liz's face the day she told me that the last word on Jesse's vocabulary list was "eternity" and how glad she was the session was ending so that she would be able to speak personally to him. Yes, he said he wanted to spend eternity with Jesus, and the angels rejoiced that day in heaven! Soon after that he wanted to go with the youth group gatherings at the church, and one event was to hear the actor Stephen Baldwin give his testimony. It was that night that Jesse publicly proclaimed Christ as his Savior! I actually got to share that with Stephen, seeing him at a shopping mall with his child a few years after Jesse had gone to heaven.

Jesse and Liz brought a lot of laughter into each other's life. Jesse was always laughing hysterically as he did not warn Liz of upcoming digestive interruptions while they sat at the table for two hours every time he was not in the hospital. I look back now and realize the importance of having had such a loyal, loving, praying friend by our side. Jesse really enjoyed going to her home with her family, sitting around her table playing board games, and getting to know her son Brian. It was a precious time for him and the beginning of an endearing friendship for me.

I know it was hard on Liz spending those three years with our family through this trial and it ending in his death. I am so grateful for her loyal friendship. I was so blessed to be a part of the small group Bible study she attended and growing in the Lord with her. She was always there for us and was the person the Lord also arranged to be at Jesse's bedside praying as he went home. She was the person I wanted with me the day I had to go pick out a casket. At the viewing she put a smile on my face by bringing Jesse a jar of gumballs as she had done so many times before to make him happy.

> And for this reason He is the Mediator of the new covenant, by means of death, for the redemption of the transgressions under the first covenant, that those who are called may receive the promise of the eternal inheritance.
>
> —HEBREWS 9:15

Dear Lord,

Thank you for the people who are obedient to the call and assignment you have given them to minister to those in need. Thank you for your divine appointments, for we know there is no such thing as coincidences. Thank you Lord for the prayer warriors, for we know that when two or three are gathered in your name, you are there with them. In the name of Jesus, Amen.

JESSE'S EIGHTH GRADE GRADUATION.

JESSE AND HIS TUTOR LIZ AT GRADUATION.

SEAN

hile Jesse was in treatment he made friends with a boy named Sean. Sean's parents were great. His dad made everyone laugh. The patients, as well as the parents, enjoyed being around that family. His mom was very sweet and quiet, yet I knew that we connected and would be special friends. Sean was a few years older than Jesse and unfortunately very experienced in all the protocols. Sean had been battling cancer on and off from the age of seven. He was such an inspiration to Jesse. He always knew the right thing to say to take away the fear. Jesse was counting on going to the town pool the upcoming weekend but was embarrassed by the lump sticking out of his chest, which was the tube that the chemo went through. He had a dilemma: do I keep a T shirt on; do I put a bandage over it; what are the girls going to say? Sean was quick to reply, "No, you don't put anything on it, and if anyone says anything you say, "I took a bullet for a woman!" I will never forget the smile on Jesse's face and the relief that he felt. Sean had the perfect solution! As the years of treatment continued, our friendships grew. When things were good with the boys, we would get together in each other's homes and just try to have some normalcy and some fun. Sean was in need of another bone marrow transplant. There was no one on the HLA Registry that even came close to matching all the properties needed to have a transplant without the risks being even greater than when you have a comparable match. Jesse had the idea that since Sean was from New Jersey and we lived in New York, we needed to look near our house for people to go on the national registry that could possibly be a match for Sean. I thought it was so sweet that despite his own battle, his love and compassion for Sean was a great concern. This was also how Sean lived his life. We contacted a local restaurant that I knew had a family member who struggled with a life-threatening illness also. They agreed to give us the time and space to host a blood and bone marrow drive. Before we knew it we were now in the mall doing the same thing. It wasn't long before the local newspapers picked up the story of this young middle school boy battling cancer trying to help his friend Sean in need. This was the beginning of what would become Jesse's Wish, his legacy that carried on enrolling over 1,000 additional people on the national registry. My son Matt was a perfect match for Jesse, but with Ewing's sarcoma they were no longer doing bone marrow transplants. No one had ever survived one. The doctor said Sean had a good chance if only they could find a match for him. It was about that time that Jesse's cancer had reoccurred, and he was now receiving more powerful double doses of chemo. There was not only lack of time to host more bone marrow drives but there was no strength or energy in either one of us. Sean continued to be a strong tower for Jesse. One particular evening very late at night, Jesse was struggling with fear and went on his computer to see if anyone was up to respond. Sean later told me how in his spirit he knew to get up and go look at his computer. He told Jesse that in the Bible there was a story about putting on the armor of God. Jesse told me what had happened that evening and somehow in my spirit I knew that this could be nearing the end of his life here, in spite of our expectancy for his physical healing.

Within that week Jesse was admitted to the hospital and overnight he became very weak; I could hardly hear him ask me, "What was the helmet for again?" That really scared me because I knew it meant the battle was happening in the spiritual realm. The next thing he whispered was "white horse." The Lord gave him a vision of a white horse! I didn't know then that it was in the book of Revelation.

I saw heaven standing open and there before me was a white horse, whose rider is called Faithful and True..." (Revelation 19:11, NIV).

Pastor Mike later talked to me more about spiritual warfare and said the enemy never stops trying to squelch the plan of God. God planned that day to be victorious and it was. Jesse took his final breath after seeing Jesus come into the room on his white horse to take him home. It was not what we had prayed for, but somehow there was an overwhelming sense of peace and assurance that he was in the arms of Jesus. Sean also brought me comfort telling me more about their last conversation, letting me know that Jesse was not afraid. He said Jesse joked about them playing baseball together in heaven as they were both huge Yankee fans.

Three years later, Sean had his transplant but not with a full match from the registry. The doctors used a partial match from umbilical cord cells. Unfortunately Sean's body rejected the transplant, and he got a horrific disease called Graft versus Host. This put him in intensive care for almost a year until he joined Jesse in heaven. It broke my heart to see his parents grieve, as I knew too well the long road before them. They continue to hold a special place in my heart as my dearest friends. I will forever be grateful for their loving support and for their son Sean's role in Jesse's life. He was a young man beyond his years, as they say, "an old soul." As his mom would say, he never wanted cancer to define him, and it never did. He always put people before himself. He accomplished so much in his brief twenty years while never complaining. Sean's older brother went on to become a doctor with an interest in cancer research as well as starting the Sean Hanna foundation. With the family's dedication and tireless efforts it has become an amazingly successful outreach supporting cancer patients and their families.

www.Seanhanna.org

> And it shall come to pass afterward, that I will pour out my Spirit on all flesh; your sons and your daughters shall prophesy, your old men shall dream dreams, and your young men shall see visions. Even on the male and female servants in those days I will pour out my Spirit.
>
> —JOEL 2:28–29, ESV

Lord,

I will be strong in you and in the strength of your might. I will put on the whole armor of God, that I may be able to stand against the schemes of the devil. For I do not wrestle against flesh and blood, but against the rulers, against the authorities, against the cosmic powers over this present darkness, against the spiritual forces of evil in the heavenly places. Therefore I take up the whole armor of God, that I may be able to withstand in the evil day, and having done all, to stand firm. Stand therefore, having fastened on the belt of truth, and having put on the breastplate of righteousness, and, as shoes for my feet, having put on the readiness given by the gospel of peace. In all circumstances I will take up the shield of faith, with which we can extinguish all the flaming darts of the evil one; and take the helmet of salvation, and the sword of the Spirit, which is the word of God, praying at all times in the Spirit, with all prayer and supplication. To that end keep alert with all perseverance, making supplication for all the saints, and also for me, that words may be given to me in opening my mouth boldly to proclaim the mystery of the gospel, for which I am an ambassador in chains, that I may declare it boldly, as I ought to speak (Ephesians 6:10–20, ESV). In the name of Jesus, Amen.

POEM MARIAN'S COUSIN WROTE AFTER HEARING THE EULOGY ABOUT JESSE'S VISION OF A WHITE HORSE (BELOW)

White Horse
in the sky

Where the heavens shine down
Soars a spirit earthbound
Unseen to a human eye
As it crosses the horizon
Only God has his eyes on
This great White Horse in the sky
One of his noblest moves
An angel on four hooves
Summoned from the Master's side
To swing open the gates
As the kingdom awaits
For Jesse on his greatest ride
Through his darkest hour
He never would cower
Stood tall and gave it a fight
Such strong discipline
From the courage within
Gave hope to a flickering light
He had such spirit
You could actually hear it
Went on with his life as desired
Showed much goodwill
Pulled for friends who were ill
Leaving many in awe and inspired
Yet all through his pain
It would not be in vain
For God had followed his course
"Jesse you've given your best
Now it's time for you to rest
Come home on that great White Horse"
So into the heavens he rode
To a celestial abode
While on earth his memory remains
"Shed me no tear
I have nothing to fear
For God is pulling my reins"

SEAN AND JESSE

Rob Carpentier

THE BOYS

J esse was my one child who you could tell belonged to me. Unlike Matt and Sami who have the dark hair and olive Italian skin like their dad, Jesse was fair like me with freckles and hazel eyes. He was a real jokester and enjoyed life to the fullest, always having many friends. At this writing it has been eleven years since Jesse's home-going, and I still hear from the boys a few times a year. They are Rob, Jay, Jake, Paul, Corey, Matty, and Anthony. They are some of the finest young men I know. They were true friends to Jesse and were crucial in sustaining his enjoyment of life during those three hard years. Rob is as big a Yankee fan as Jesse was, and so they went to several games together. They shared a love of sports and video games. They played soccer together for many years. After Jesse's home-going Rob always made sure that the boys got together for his birthday at our house. They would each talk about their favorite memory of Jesse.

Jay just recently sent me a picture of his leather bracelet inscribed "SPINA" as they liked to call Jesse. I know Jay had a tough time grieving, and he kept in touch with me confessing his struggle getting through college. He admitted that he had dabbled with drugs as most kids their age were doing. He seems to have a great life now with a good job and a nice girl in his life. Paul was another one who turned to drugs. Paul's mom is a good friend of mine, and I hurt for her. He is such a smart kid and could do so much with his life. I'm not saying that any of this was a result of their losing Jesse, but it didn't help. Paul is doing great now and working to help others stay straight.

Jake really struggled with seeing Jesse go through his treatment, especially having firsthand knowledge since his dad Michael suffered with cancer also. Jake wrote our family a beautiful letter the day after Jesse's home-going saying how much he loved Jesse, and that he was his role model, his best friend, one of the funniest and strongest kids he knew, and that he would make sure he would not be forgotten. Jake's dad Michael was an amazing man and friend to me. He supported us by not just attending our blood/bone marrow drives, but by sitting with us throughout the entire event. He was a man a faith and enjoyed talking with my pastor about God. Michael died soon after Jesse. I will never forget leaving Jesse's burial site and looking back out the window of the car that Michael was the last one standing there.

Corey was the one I think was most like Jesse, having that emotional side and love of music. They would both spend time together learning the guitar. Anthony is Jesse's cousin, so they were together since they were toddlers. He got very close to Corey and they actually roomed together in college and have both now moved to Nevada to work.

I'll never forget the last Halloween party Jesse had at our house. He wanted this ugly scary mask that I didn't want to spend forty dollars for. Well, I did anyway and of course he never wore it. He decided, after seeing Matty walk in dressed as a girl, that he had to become one too. So there he went, into my closet, putting on my black sequin dress and high heels, spinning around and falling down laughing!

The boys also formed a team for "Jesse's Wish" to be represented at several cancer events including Lymphoma and Leukemia

Association and American Cancer Society where Jesse entered as a survivor after his first trial of chemo. It was so funny because the participants were supposed to walk the high school track, but Jesse ran as soon as the ribbon fell! So of course he won the walk and his story was written up in the local newspaper. The local newspapers continually covered Jesse's Wish Drives telling the story of the boy who was trying to help his friend with cancer find a bone marrow match while still in treatment himself. Jesse's friends were a big part of the success of those drives, posting flyers, fundraising at their school, and getting people to attend.

Jesse had a great math teacher named Brian who went out of his way to come to our house to tutor Jesse in Math. Brian soon became like one of the boys. He loved Jesse and although he was a busy young man and planning his wedding, he spent time with Jesse beyond the schoolwork, taking him in his red sports car to play video games and race cars. When Brian did get married, he placed a photo of Jesse on the table alongside of his guests' seating assignments to make them aware of "Jesse's Wish." He planned a memorial service at the school where they planted a tree and placed an inscribed baseball plaque, which still remains. Jesse's youth pastor, Jim spoke there that day where I know hearts were touched and seeds were planted, not just a tree.

> Now the parable is this: The seed is the word of God.
>
> —LUKE 8:11, ESV

> As for that in the good soil, they are those who, hearing the word, hold it fast in an honest and good heart, and bear fruit with patience.
>
> —LUKE 8:15, ESV

For the one who sows to his own flesh will from the flesh reap corruption, but the one who sows to the Spirit will from the Spirit reap eternal life.

—GALATIANS 6:8, ESV

To know wisdom and instruction, to understand words of insight, to receive instruction in wise dealing, in righteousness, justice, and equity; to give prudence to the simple, knowledge and discretion to the youth—Let the wise hear and increase in learning, and the one who understands obtain guidance, to understand a proverb and a saying, the words of the wise and their riddles.

—PROVERBS 1:1–6, ESV

Dear Lord,

I thank you so much for these young men and the role that you assigned in their lives for Jesse. I pray that your living water pour over them to grow those seeds in their life so that they will become the men you created them to be; that they would know that they have value and purpose. I thank you that you have shown them how fragile this life is but that they have the opportunity to accept the finished work of the cross of your son Jesus and that through Him they can have eternal life and thereby see Jesse again. In the name of Jesus, Amen.

JESSE HOLDING HIS AWARD FOR COURAGE
AND CITIZENSHIP AT HIS GRADUATION

TABLE SET UP AT TEACHER BRIAN'S WEDDING

9/11

It had only been about two months since we began waking up at six every morning. I would pretty much have to carry Jesse into the car half-asleep and drive into New York City for, as his doctor put it, "a full-time job" from 7:30 AM to 6:30 PM every day. I was glad that we lived only thirty miles from one of the top cancer hospitals in the world. I would listen to Pastor Charles Stanley on the radio for strength and encouragement to live through these days that seemed like a bad nightmare. One of the nurses knew that Jesse loved the New York Yankees and offered us tickets for an afternoon game and said that we could come by after the game for his chemo. That was September 11, 2001, one of the most horrible days in the history of this country. I couldn't even bring myself to look at it on television. That compounded with Jesse's illness made me wonder whether this was the end of the world. I knew in my heart that God kept us from being in the middle of that mess that day, yet it wasn't until years later that I actually thanked Him for that. Days later we were finally able to receive a letter from the hospital to show the soldier at the George Washington Bridge that we had permission to go into the city. I just remember feeling that this couldn't really be happening. Now the thirty mile, forty-five minute drive took hours coming home each day with trying to weave back into the traffic after having to pull off for Jesse to be sick. The hospital had taken in victims due to lack of space in other hospitals and it was even more chaotic than it had been before. Crying, confusion, and a sense of hopelessness were everywhere. One of the moms that I had met who had a son going through treatment lost her nephew that day. I'll never forget the fear and dread on her face.

Yet we read that this was also a time of revival in the churches, however short-lived. There were many conversations on how God could allow something like this. It gave me even more reason to dig into His Word and try to understand that for myself. I became known in the hospital as the woman with the Bible. That was okay with me because I knew it was giving me strength. For the first time my heart was being lifted up. It wasn't just words I was reading. I knew then that it was God speaking to me. I was compelled to share the peace I was beginning to receive and was filled with compassion for others. It was taking my complete focus off of my circumstances and trying to help others that increased my peace and gave me strength.

> "If my people who are called by my name humble themselves, and pray and seek my face and turn from their wicked ways, then I will hear from heaven and will forgive their sin and heal their land"
>
> —2 CHRONICLES 7:14, ESV

> Blessed be the God and Father of our Lord Jesus Christ, the Father of mercies and God of all comfort, who comforts us in all our affliction, so that we may be able to comfort those who are in any affliction, with the comfort with which we ourselves are comforted by God. For as we share abundantly in Christ's sufferings, so through Christ we share abundantly in comfort too. If we

are afflicted, it is for your comfort and salvation; and if we are comforted, it is for your comfort, which you experience when you patiently endure the same sufferings that we suffer. Our hope for you is unshaken, for we know that as you share in our sufferings, you will also share in our comfort.

—2 CORINTHIANS 1:3–7, ESV

That the God of our Lord Jesus Christ, the Father of glory, may give you the Spirit of wisdom and of revelation in the knowledge of him, having the eyes of your hearts enlightened, that you may know what is the hope to which he has called you, what are the riches of his glorious inheritance in the saints, and what is the immeasurable greatness of his power toward us who believe, according to the working of his great might that he worked in Christ when he raised him from the dead and seated him at his right hand in the heavenly places, far above all rule and authority and power and dominion, and above every name that is named, not only in this age but also in the one to come. And he put all things under his feet and gave him as head over all things to the church, which is his body, the fullness of him who fills all in all.

—EPHESIANS 1:17–23, ESV

Hannah
and Luke

Recently I had been recalling stories in my mind of the wonderful moms that I met during the three years of Jesse's hospital treatment. One mom who came back into my heart was Hannah. We have been in touch over these past eleven years once or twice a year. She would always reach out to me on Mother's Day and Christmas. As my thoughts were on her this week, I received a call from her, and yet it's not either of those holidays. She felt she wanted to share something with me, unsure of how I would react. She prefaced it by saying she had never been to a fortune teller or a medium but she was at a party where there was a man who contacted angels and reported what our loved ones wanted to say to us. He told her about a boy she knew and loved that wanted to give her a message for his mother. His initials were JS and his mom's name started with an M. She felt the chills go down her arms and listened intently. His report was that the boy wanted his mom to know that she made the right decision. I just laughed and said to Hannah, "Well at least I made a good decision." I began to tell her what the Bible says about angels, and that Jesse was not an angel. It gave me an opportunity to speak God's love for her—that He wanted to speak to her, and He knew she was seeking answers.

Hannah admitted that she was ready to take the next step, knowing she was unfulfilled with the "religion" she had grown up with. She said she had started to listen to Charles Stanley. I told her that was a great place to start but most importantly she needed to see what God had to say to her through His Word. I recommended a study bible and told her I would pray for the trial she was now facing. She also went through a terrible divorce as a result of issues that surfaced when her son was going through treatment for Leukemia. They actually have a statistic that concludes that four out of five marriages do not survive the death of a child. Of the twenty-nine families that I met during Jesse's three-year battle with cancer, unfortunately, many of those marriages did not make it. That fact gives me something else to pray about.

Hannah's son Luke was only four years old when he and Jesse met in the hospital. Hannah recalled that first time we met in this recent phone conversation, and it's funny how I have no recollection of that day. She said I approached her about signing a petition to get government support for childhood cancer funding. Her first thought was that here I was with such an ill son, and yet I was trying to help other children there; she told me that that impressed her. The next time we saw each other she could recall the exact date, July 31, because it was the day she was told that her son's cancer was much more progressed than they had thought, and that he would need more intense treatment. She said she could not help herself from crying uncontrollably to the point of not even being able to take care of her son when Jesse and I stepped into the room. Jesse called Luke a "dude" and at that young age he thought that it was so funny. He told his mom that Jesse always made him laugh. Hannah apologized for not attending Jesse's funeral saying she couldn't bear to see him that way. I told her don't even think you need to apologize. She went on to tell me how much Luke talked about Jesse for so many years later until she finally told her son that Jesse was in heaven. This young man went on to write a story about Jesse for a competition, winning

$2,500, which he put into Jesse's foundation. He continues to raise money for cancer attributing his passion to "a friend who encouraged him named Jesse." He was even filmed in a commercial for the local blood center testifying to that very thing. Hannah heard Jesse say to Luke that when he grew up he should do everything he could to help kids with cancer. It amazes me to hear this now, and yet it does not surprise me that God used Jesse to utter a prophetic word to a four-year-old child who has carried that to fruition. Luke always made Jesse smile too. He loved sitting on the bed with him. He taught him how to play video games to take his mind off of where he was.

God is so good. He also knew this week I needed encouragement from remembering painful things from the past and knowing that the enemy of our soul likes to attack us when we are glorifying God. Praise to you Lord that you who are in us is greater than he who is in the world! There are no coincidences in this world. I'm grateful, knowing God was using me to speak truth into Hannah's heart. He will bring revelation to her through His Word. He wants to reveal truth in your life! My heart is so filled with joy knowing the journey that Hannah is about to embark on will be the greatest time of her life. I feel privileged to cover her in prayer as she begins to read the greatest story ever told and learn God's plan for her life.

> He will command his angels concerning you, to guard you.
>
> —LUKE 4:10, ESV

> At that time the disciples came to Jesus, saying, "Who is the greatest in the kingdom of heaven?" And calling to him a child, he put him in the midst of them and said, "Truly, I say to you, unless you turn and become like children, you will never enter the kingdom of heaven. Whoever

humbles himself like this child is the greatest in the kingdom of heaven.

—MATTHEW 18:1–4, ESV

And there appeared to him an angel from heaven, strengthening him.

—LUKE 22:43, ESV

Dear Lord,

Thank you for the gift of children. Thank you for their spirit of innocence and example of faith that we need to emulate. Thank you for those who use their suffering to help others in need, bringing about change and awareness. In the name of Jesus, Amen.

MARYLAND

In October 2002 Jesse's doctor said he saw a new spot on the PET scan and that he felt the best course of action, since his cancer had come back after the first protocol, would be a bone marrow transplant at the National Cancer Institute in Maryland. They weren't yet performing transplants in New York for his type of cancer. We made the decision to go to Maryland and drove in our car in spite of reported sniper shootings that were taking place in that direct area for over three weeks where seventeen people were killed and ten were injured. I could remember not even being afraid of that because what my son was facing seemed far graver and more imminent than being shot by a sniper. I do however remember the fear of whether he would live through this bone marrow transplant and how very alone the two of us felt in that strange place with so many uncertainties lying before us. The day after we arrived they wanted to do another PET scan to which I replied, "Why can't you just go by the one that New York sent to you?" Jesse had been through so much poking and prodding and tests that I tried to save him from one more, but they did not agree. So now my precious boy was again stuck in a loud, narrow, long tube trying to keep still while they fixed their cameras on his internal organs. I sat again in yet another cold sterile room reading God's Word, praying the Psalms back to him; waiting for Him to answer my prayer for my son's healing. We had been in these cold loud rooms many times before in New York as scans were required every month for a ninety-minute study to determine the cancer's progression. Somehow this day felt different. I left that room with a hope I had not had before. That hope was realized as the doctor read us the report the next day. They said they did not see anything on the PET scan; therefore, they would not be performing the transplant. The only way that they could explain it was that there was possibly either juice or a urine spot on his hospital gown when they did the last scan in New York. I just smiled and thought to myself, *you can believe that but I know what really happened*! They went on to say that we could take the next small plane back to New York that day. I remember grabbing Jesse's hand, running through that hospital corridor back to our room to grab our things and catch the next plane. I knew that I knew that I knew that this was a miracle! Those kinds of mistakes just don't happen. As we got settled in our seats on the plane I began to pray, thanking the Lord for what I knew He had just done. I was thinking about where I wanted to read in the Bible and decided to go to the scripture given in my daily devotional dated Friday, October 25, and it was very appropriately titled, "Tested by Fire." Can the fiery trials of life actually prove to be a blessing? The apostle Peter indicated to us that they could. He explained that various trials could result in "praise, glory and honor when Jesus Christ is revealed" (1 Peter 1: 6–7, NIV). "Fiery trials may be very painful, but if by God's grace we endure them, our faith can emerge from the blazing furnace purer and stronger than it was before" (Vernon Grounds). That, no doubt, was a very powerful word to me from the Lord, and further confirmation that it was directly for me in that particular moment—I later realized I was on the wrong date of my devotional.

I ripped that page out of the devotional to always be a reminder to me of what the Lord did for us that day. It is now eleven years later as I hold this little devotional page in my hand in awe of our amazing God and how He carried us through that trial giving us hope when we needed it most! I believe it wasn't yet his appointed time. The Lord didn't want us in the middle of sniper crossfire or in a strange state away from our family and friends. It was just not the time appointed for Jesse to go home to the Lord. I'm grateful that He got us out of there and gave me two more years with my son.

The devotional concluded with this poem: "Some through the waters, some through the flood,/Some through the fire, but all through the blood;/Some through great sorrow, but God gives a song, in the night season and all the daylong" (G.A. Young).

> But he knows the way that I take; when he has tested me, I shall come out as gold.
>
> —JOB 23:10, ESV

> If that *is the case*, our God whom we serve is able to deliver us from the burning fiery furnace, and He will deliver *us* from your hand, O king. But if not, let it be known to you, O king, that we do not serve your gods, nor will we worship the gold image which you have set up.
>
> —DANIEL 3:17–18

Dear Lord,

Thank you that you carry us through our trials and refine us so that we become more like your son Jesus. Thank you that we can learn from our trials how much we need you and can't live without you—that we are your beloved children and you are a good, good father. Help us to keep our eyes focused on you so that we are more and more aware of your hand on our lives at all times. In the name of Jesus, Amen.

The Angel in the Bahamas

My body still trembles when I remember hearing the words from the doctor that we should take Jesse on vacation since there was nothing more he could do. Jesse always wanted to swim with the dolphins. We loved the Bahamas. We had taken Matt there when he was three years old, but Jesse and Sami had never been there. We chose the most beautiful hotel called the Atlantis, which had an aquarium attraction that was so exciting to Jesse. He could swim through a tube in the midst of the fish. You would never know that he had only weeks left on this earth, according to the doctors. Without the chemo in his body he seemed like a normal healthy child. He was having a lot of fun and I was doing my best to keep my hope that the doctors were not right and that the only true physician is Jesus Christ.

One afternoon when the boys were resting up in the room, I took a walk with my daughter along the beach. I invited their dad to join us, and he said, "No, I'll just wait here," and sat on the sand. Sami and

I walked up to these old ruins where there were many steps leading to a small platform right at the foot of the water. I remember feeling a little uncomfortable at some of the young men that were hanging out at the bottom of the steps almost blocking our way and staring at us as we approached. Yet I remember feeling determined to walk past them anyway, wanting to see the view from the top. When we got to the top there was one man who said hello. He appeared to be a native of the island. As I looked out at the huge hotel, I spoke to the man saying that I read that people pay thousands of dollars just to stay one night on the upper floors of that hotel. He said, "Yes, that's right." I told him I thought that was crazy. It is such a waste of money when there are children dying of cancer due to lack of funding for research. I shared with him that my son was fighting cancer and there were only five drugs known for his type of cancer in the best hospital in the country. He said he was sorry to hear that and asked if it would be okay if he prayed. Before I knew it he had grabbed my hand and my daughters, raised them up to the sky and began to utter one of the most anointed prayers I had ever heard. Being new to the Word of God, I wasn't familiar with God being referred to as "Jesus of Nazareth, the Alpha and the Omega," as he began praying. I remember thinking that my daughter's arms were probably getting tired, and I should get back to the boys, but I knew something special was happening. When the praying was over I asked if he wouldn't mind if I took a picture of him to remember. He obliged, and we then walked back to the beach to Sam's dad. I began to tell him what had occurred, and he looked strangely at me as he said he saw us there but no one else. On the way home in the plane I looked up the scripture in Revelation 21 that the man had prayed. I developed the pictures as soon as we got home, anxious to look at him again and to my surprise that picture was not there. In my heart I knew he was an angel. I had never believed that something like that could and would happen, but I now know what the Bible says is true, and I have no doubt that God sent that angel to me as I was struggling and in need of encouragement. I also believe that those men that made me uncomfortable at the foot of the steps were the attempt of the enemy trying to keep me from what God had for me. This was a lesson and memory I recall anytime fear tries to avert my walk with the Lord. Jesus commanded us to not be afraid. In fact, I read that the command is in the Bible 365 times! That's enough reason for me. We need to fight the good fight and remember the battle is already won.

> "For God has not given us a spirit of fear, but of power and of love and of a sound mind"
>
> —2 TIMOTHY 1:7

> But now, thus says the LORD, who created you, O Jacob, And He who formed you, O Israel: "Fear not, for I have redeemed you; I have called *you* by your name; You *are* Mine."
>
> —ISAIAH 43:1

> Yea, though I walk through the valley of the shadow of death, I will fear no evil; For You *are* with me; Your rod and Your staff, they comfort me.
>
> —PSALM 23:4

> Have I not commanded you? Be strong and of good courage; do not be afraid, nor be dismayed, for the LORD your God *is* with you wherever you go.
>
> —JOSHUA 1:9

> Are not all angels ministering spirits sent to serve those who will inherit salvation?
>
> —HEBREWS 1:14, NIV

Dear Lord,

Thank you for sending your ministering spirits to encourage us. Thank you for the angel who encouraged me and showed me how to pray in the spirit. I am in awe of you. You are the Alpha and Omega, the beginning and the end. You are the same yesterday, today, and tomorrow. You are faithful! Thank you that there is not a day, a need that comes, where you are not present to give us exactly what we need. I honor you, praise you, and give you all the glory. In the name of Jesus, Amen.

THE ORTHODOX DOCTOR

Receiving treatment for cancer in one of the world's leading hospitals has its advantages as well as disadvantages. One of the disadvantages, besides feeling like just a number—a statistic, data for their clinical trials—is sometimes dealing with some of the doctors who were just very abrupt. They are brilliant, and I suppose they get somewhat burned out, overwhelmed, and probably need to detach personally. I learned how to be an advocate for my son and to not be intimidated by their poor bedside manner. One day a Jewish orthodox doctor crossed the line. He told me that I needed to tell Jesse the three possible scenarios on how he was going to die so that he would know what to expect. He said he's fourteen years old, and that he's old enough to understand. Not only were those three scenarios so horrific that I could not even bring myself to repeat them, I looked at him and said, "Absolutely not." I will not tell my child any such thing and neither will you. My faith tells me that Jesus can heal my son at any time and that is the hope that we hold on to. Of course he was not happy with my reply and became even more difficult. Most mornings, not knowing if he was the one I was going to have to see when we checked in became very stressful.

Jesse's primary doctor at least told us that he was stopping treatment and to take him on vacation—to enjoy these last weeks together.

The weekend came very quickly when we needed to be back for blood transfusions, with no indication that it would be the last time I would ever have to bring Jesse there. The nurses spent a great deal of time convincing me to sign a "do not resuscitate" order that Friday evening. The next day the nurses were telling him that they needed to put a catheter in and Jesse asked, "It's not permanent is it?" *No Jesse*, I thought to myself, *our bodies, this life, death, it is not permanent*! Friends and family began to gather around his bed, kneeling down and praying aloud when in walked the orthodox doctor. That day, of course, it didn't cross my mind that he was there on a Saturday, as never before, being it was their Sabbath. Now it is very clear that the Lord wanted him there. He heard the prayers, heard the hymns, while he stood comforting my daughter with his arm around her. He lifted the tubes out of the way to help me get in the bed with Jesse. He heard me tell Jesse that I loved him and that Jesus loved him so: "Don't be afraid." I told him that Jesus was there to take him to his true home on that white horse, and that I would see him again very soon. Jesse never experienced any of those three horrific scenarios. He took his last breath peacefully in what I can only describe as an atmosphere heavily surrounded by the manifest presence of God!

I wrote a letter to that doctor thanking him for his kindness and compassion that he showed that day, and I inserted it in a New Testament Bible in Hebrew. I will never know the outcome of the seeds that were planted in his heart that day, but I know that he may very possibly be one of those people I get to see in heaven.

One of Jesse's main nurses was off that day but came in when she heard what was happening and later said to me that what she witnessed there was one of the most peaceful deaths that she had seen there in her twelve years on that pediatric floor. With the amount of children that are treated there, the number sometimes reached three deaths a week.

> So I ask, did they stumble in order that they might fall? By no means! Rather through their trespass salvation has come to the Gentiles, so as to make Israel jealous. Now if their trespass means riches for the world, and if their failure means riches for the Gentiles, how much more will their full inclusion mean! Now I am speaking to you Gentiles. Inasmuch then as I am an apostle to the Gentiles, I magnify my ministry in order somehow to make my fellow Jews jealous, and thus save some of them. For if their rejection means the reconciliation of the world, what will their acceptance mean but life from the dead? If the dough offered as firstfruits is holy, so is the whole lump, and if the root is holy, so are the branches.
>
> —ROMANS 11:11–16, ESV

One of the many treasures Pastor Mike shared with me after Jesse's home-going was "sometimes God takes the first fruits." In the Bible Jesse is the father of King David. I had no idea when I named Jesse what his name represented Biblically. I am so overjoyed to know now and to see how Jesse's life is bearing fruit for the kingdom!

> And again Isaiah says, 'The root of Jesse will come, even he who arises to rule the Gentiles; in him will the Gentiles hope.' May the God of hope fill you with all joy and peace in believing, so that

by the power of the Holy Spirit you may abound in hope.

—ROMANS 15:12–13, ESV

There shall come forth a shoot from the stump of Jesse, and a branch from his roots shall bear fruit. And the Spirit of the LORD shall rest upon him, the Spirit of wisdom and understanding, the Spirit of counsel and might, the Spirit of knowledge and the fear of the LORD.

—ISAIAH 11:1–2, ESV

Thank you Lord for sending your son Jesus. Thank you for Saul of Tarsus who you named Paul, a Jew who was persecuting Christians before you transformed his heart on the road to Damascus. Thank you for giving him revelation to write two thirds of your Word having never even witnessed your miracles on earth. He knew in his heart who you were and that we no longer needed the law because Jesus fulfilled it and covered us with His grace. In the name of Jesus, Amen.

DAVE
PETTIGREW

J esse was starting to like girls. There was one particular sweet and bubbly girl named Jamie. I met her parents, who were very gracious to us. Jamie's dad Richard invited me to a Christmas concert at their church. Members of the band grew up in the area, had attended that church, and came back every year for this performance. The female vocalist had an amazing voice that melted my heart as she sang, "Mary Did You Know?" She also performed another song called "Mary's Shoes." I didn't know then how much those words would mean to me, being a mom watching her child suffer as Mary did with Jesus. The band's leader, Dave Pettigrew, noticed I signed my email as "Thirddaypraise," which started a conversation about the band it was named after and my love for music. Dave then realized that I was Richard's friend. He knew about Jesse from Richard, and Dave told me that he had linked "Jesse's Wish" website to his webpage to help bring about awareness. I thought that was such an amazing thing to do, never having ever met us. Being a young dad and a strong Christian man who loves to worship the Lord through song, I'm sure he felt compassion for Jesse and me.

The first time I heard Dave sing the words to his song, "Are you really listening?" I was moved to tears because I knew that I had asked God that very same question, and like Dave, I know He not only listens—He really cares! When Dave sang, "If You Show Me the Way, I Will Follow," all I could do was shout "*Amen!*" He not only shows us the way, He comes with us! After Jesse went home to be with the Lord I was very comforted listening to Dave's music. I invited him to play at our church one evening. I was nervous there wouldn't be a good turnout for him, and it was just a small group, yet Dave's words to me were so true: "If one soul is saved, if one heart is renewed, that's enough for me." With a heart like that I knew God would bless him and sure enough, his ministry has grown. He is an amazing advocate for "World Vision," a Christian humanitarian organization sponsoring children in need. He has now opened up for popular Christian bands and is on "The Message" satellite radio. One particular song, "There is Hope," which is a tribute to 9/11, amazingly expresses the promises of God to give us hope. Hope—isn't that what we all need, even if we don't know what we're hoping for, and for some people, who they are hoping in? I made an acronym for the word HOPE—Having Overwhelming Peace Every-day! I don't know what you might be going through right now, but in 2 Corinthians 4:17–18, His word says: For our light affliction, which is but for a moment, is working for us a far more exceeding *and* eternal weight of glory, while we do not look at the things which are seen, but at the things which are not seen. For the things which are seen *are* temporary, but the things, which *are* not seen are eternal.

How glorious to see from where the Lord has brought me, and where He's bringing me! He did it for me, and He wants to do it for you!

Let worship music penetrate your soul and bring you into His presence! We were created to worship Him.

Please pray to consider helping Dave in this trustworthy ministry. Please log on to Davepettigrew.net or sponsorachildnow.net

For his anger lasts only a moment, but his favor lasts a lifetime; weeping may stay for the night, but rejoicing comes in the morning.

—PSALMS 30:5, NIV

Be strong and courageous. Do not be afraid or terrified because of them, for the LORD your God goes with you; he will never leave you nor forsake you.

—DEUTERONOMY 31:6, NIV

Therefore, since we have been justified by faith, we have peace with God through our Lord Jesus Christ. Through him we have also obtained access by faith into this grace in which we stand, and we rejoice in hope of the glory of God. Not only that, but we rejoice in our sufferings, knowing that suffering produces endurance, and endurance produces character, and character produces hope, and hope does not put us to shame, because God's love has been poured into our hearts through the Holy Spirit who has been given to us.

—ROMANS 5:1–5, ESV

If I give all I possess to the poor and give over my body to hardship that I may boast, but do not have love, I gain nothing.

—1 CORINTHIANS 13:3, NIV

For in this hope we were saved. But hope that is seen is no hope at all. Who hopes for what they already have? But if we hope for what we do not yet have, we wait for it patiently.

—ROMANS 8:24–25, NIV

Abba Father,

Thank you for those who give of their time and talent to help those in need. I pray for an outpouring of your spirit on children who wait on those who are more fortunate to give to their needs. For it is in giving that we receive. Thank you for the spark of revival we witnessed in the churches after 9/11. I pray for more, Lord! May your Holy Spirit bring revival in our homes, in our churches, and sweep though our nation, that we will return to being "one nation under God." In the name of Jesus, Amen.

RACHAEL

I was so grateful that Jesse came up with the idea to host blood and bone marrow drives in our community to help his friends he met at the hospital find a match. After he went home to be with the Lord, my friend Rachael said to me, "You should continue hosting the drives in Jesse's memory; it could be his legacy." It was just what I needed, having lost my role as caregiver—pouring myself completely into Jesse getting well, and it was now over. I used that energy to possibly help save other lives by hosting as many blood and bone marrow drives as needed, and oh are they needed. They say that four out of five people are touched by cancer in their lives. Since "Jesse's Wish" began in 2004, about 1,200 people have been added to the national registry at our drives. Though it is not always possible to track results from individual drives, we know of seven matches that have resulted from "Jesse's Wish" drives. This is clearly the hand of God because even though there are ten million people on the national registry, it is estimated that 6,000 people every day are searching for a match. There is only a 30 percent chance that even a family member will match.

Rachael had been part of "Jesse's Wish" drives from the beginning and was instrumental in organizing the blood drives and continuing Jesse's Wish. She always made sure what the posters said was a testament to Jesse's compassionate heart for his friends, and always made sure I liked the picture she used. She stayed and sat with me at many drives when she didn't have to be there. I felt a strong connection to her. She is a strong, hardworking professional Jewish woman who showed me much compassion. I felt like the Lord had something in mind for us as friends but couldn't imagine what that would look like. Rachael nominated me for an award given by the local blood center after several drives were held. The award I received was a beautiful glass globe with an inscription, "You Mean the World to Us." Rachael made a speech about Jesse and how I, as his mom, was carrying on this legacy. I remember feeling unaffected by the accolade, thinking that I didn't want notoriety, I just want my son back, when Rachael got to the last line of her speech quoting J.R.R. Tolkien: "Faithless is he that says farewell when the road darkens." In that moment she was reminding me that yes, I have faith I need to hold on to—a faith that gives me hope. "Now faith is the substance of things hoped for, the evidence of things not seen" (Hebrews 11:1, KJV). I needed to acknowledge my pain and do what it says in His Word in 1 Peter 5:7: "casting all your cares upon Him, for He cares for you."

I needed to believe His word. "God blesses those who mourn, for they will be comforted" (Matthew 5:4, NLT).

Even though Rachael and I did not share the same beliefs, I know she respected mine and was open to hear my stories. I told her about my Jewish neighbor Eileen who came up to me outside one day and said, "I don't know how you do it every day. I see you leaving with your son before the sun comes up and coming home so late every day. Did you know I have cancer? It is breast cancer that has metastasized." I told her I was sorry to hear that, and I would pray for her. Her response was, "I've always wondered if Jesus was the Messiah." I replied joyfully, "He is!"

The next day I called my pastor and asked what I could give her to read and he recommend the book *A Case for Christ* by Lee

Strobel. Soon after I gave Eileen the book, Jesse passed away. The next time I saw Eileen was at Jesse's funeral. I watched her walk out of my church from the limousine window as we waited for the car line to form for the cemetery. I could see her expression. She looked so overwhelmed and her hands were shaking. I hoped she was all right. Only a few months had gone by, and I was sitting Shiva for Eileen. Her husband told me she appreciated me giving her the book and he was returning it to me with a book she had ordered that was recommend by the author of the book I gave her. It was the New Testament! I was thrilled to know she had gone further in her search for the truth. A few weeks later as I walked my neighborhood praying, I asked God if Eileen was with Him in heaven and as sure as He gave me ears to hear, the chimes on Eileen's front porch that I had never heard before rung out.

I hope that hearing about Eileen planted a seed to perhaps have Racheal seek also—seek to know the Savior who came to give us the ultimate sacrifice. Though theological differences remain today between Christians and Jews, I believe that will change. After all, we both acknowledge one God, Jehovah, the God of Abraham, and He is in control. Sadly, I now know one of the reasons that God brought Rachael into my life. Her twenty-year-old son recently committed suicide while at college studying to be a doctor. Needless to say it was quite a shock, not knowing he was suffering from depression. It breaks my heart knowing what she and her family are going through. I'm reminded of a song I heard by Hillsong, "The Love of God is Stronger than the Power of Death." I hope I portray that I am living proof of that. I want to share His love with Rachael and as a mom who understands her pain, let her know that she will be all right. I'd like to talk about the story of Job with her in hopes that she will see that although God does allow suffering, He is a redeeming God.

I recently read that Rachael is channeling her passion and energy now to help prevent other families from this horrific shock. She has gone to her senator, presented a bill to him that has now been signed, establishing Mental Illness Anti-Stigma Fund into law!

But those who hope in the LORD will renew their strength. They will soar on wings like eagles; they will run and not grow weary, they will walk and not be faint.

—ISAIAH 40:31, NIV

After Job had prayed for his friends, the LORD restored his fortunes and gave him twice as much as he had before.

—JOB 42:10, NIV

Who has believed what he has heard from us? And to whom has the arm of the Lord been revealed? For he grew up before him like a young plant, and like a root out of dry ground; he had no form or majesty that we should look at him, and no beauty that we should desire him. He was despised and rejected by men; a man of sorrows, and acquainted with grief; and as one from whom men hide their faces he was despised, and we esteemed him not. Surely he has borne our griefs and carried our sorrows; yet we esteemed him stricken, smitten by God, and afflicted. But he was pierced for our transgressions; he was crushed for our iniquities; upon him was the chastisement that brought us peace, and with his wounds we are healed.

—ISAIAH 53:1–5, ESV

They will be called the Holy People, the Redeemed of the Lord; and you will be called Sought After, the City No Longer Deserted.

—ISAIAH 62:12, NIV

In the past God spoke to our ancestors through the prophets at many times and in various ways, but in these last days he has spoken to us by his Son, whom he appointed heir of all things, and through whom also he made the universe. The Son is the radiance of God's glory and the exact representation of his being, sustaining all things by his powerful word. After he had provided purification for sins, he sat down at the right hand of the Majesty in heaven.

—HEBREWS 1:1–3, NIV

Father God,

I thank you for your promises for Israel. Thank you for all spiritual wisdom and understanding so that we will bear fruit and respond to the prophetic call in the last days. Thank you for your protective care. LORD, deepen our desire to share your saving power with everyone and pour out a spirit of grace and supplication so that many will have a full revelation of who you are. In the name of Jesus, Amen.

MICHAEL

My nephew Michael had been struggling with drug addiction when Jesse was diagnosed with cancer. He said to me, "I'm killing myself with these drugs and that poor kid has no control over what's happening to him. I'm going to clean myself up, see if my girl will have me back, ask her to marry me, and have Jesse be in the wedding." I'm thrilled to say that actually all came to be. It was such a great day. Jesse looked so handsome in his tux with his hair starting to grow back. He was such a beautiful boy inside and out.

Looking back Michael was probably the first person whose life was transformed by God because of Jesse. My sister had been keeping in the pain of watching her son's addiction to heroin for four years! Below is a letter Michael wrote to me as a tribute to what Jesse had done for him.

> When I found out Jesse had cancer, I was concerned but needless to say indifferent. I was going through my own struggle with addiction and took a rather nonchalant attitude toward the news.
>
> It wasn't until I saw him fighting for his life that I

realized that I was wasting mine. He was fighting to live, and I was fighting to die. That was an eye opener for me, and because of that I vowed to do everything that I possibly could to get clean.

I promised Jesse that we would fight to get better together, and he would be in my wedding. He was so excited. He fought the good fight and stood in my wedding, but sadly we lost him two years later.

I remember asking my mom how God could spare me but not Jesse. It just did not seem fair.

My mom told me, "No one will ever really know the answer to that question, but one thing I do know is that we all have a purpose here in this life.... And one of Jesse's was to help you." That gave me some comfort. But I never understood why. I don't think I ever will.

Without him I would not have realized the value of my life and how I was squandering it. There is not a day that goes by that I do not think of Jesse and the gift of sight he gave me so many years ago, and for that I will always be grateful, with a heart full of love for him.

Love,
Michael

I will always have a special place in my heart for Michael. It brings me such joy to see what God has done for him and to know that He used Jesse to open his eyes and heart. I know God has a special plan for Michael's life, and I look forward to seeing that plan unfold. God has created each one of us for a purpose and has given us each an assignment. Whether we choose to accept that call on our lives and walk out our destiny is up to us.

I know I myself sometimes want to just "take the easy road" and not have the enemy bother me with lies. You know he only bothers with those who want to glorify God! I may hear him, but I ignore him, knowing he's nothing but a liar and a thief who is trying to destroy me. Yes, trying he may but succeeding he won't! I walk in victory because of Jesus who already paid the price for me!

> For though we walk in the flesh, we are not waging war according to the flesh. For the weapons of our warfare are not of the flesh but have divine power to destroy strongholds.
>
> —2 CORINTHIANS 10:3–4, ESV

> The thief comes only to steal and kill and destroy; I have come that they may have life, and have it to the full.
>
> —JOHN 10:10, NIV

> But you belong to God, my dear children. You have already won a victory over those people, because the Spirit who lives in you is greater than the spirit who lives in the world.
>
> —1 JOHN 4:4, NLT

> But in our time something new has been added. What Moses and the prophets witnessed to all those years has happened. The God-setting-things-right that we read about has become Jesus-

setting-things-right for us. And not only for us, but for everyone who believes in him. For there is no difference between them and us in this. Since we've compiled this long and sorry record as sinners (both us and them) and proved that we are utterly incapable of living the glorious lives God wills for us, God did it for us. Out of sheer generosity he put us in right standing with himself. A pure gift. He got us out of the mess we're in and restored us to where he always wanted us to be. And he did it by means of Jesus Christ.

—ROMANS 3:21–24, MSG

Lord,

Forgive us for the times we have sinned against you and have not used our bodies as living sacrifices to you. Thank you for emptying our vessels of the things that are not of you. We bind the spirit of addiction in the name of the Lord Jesus Christ and we loose your Spirit in our lives. Lord, please heal our bodies—for you are the Great Physician—that we may be strengthened in order to serve you while we wait for your return. In the name of Jesus, Amen.

JESSE AT HIS COUSIN
MICHAEL'S WEDDING

DARLENE

Pastor Jentezen Franklin wrote a book called *Right Place, Right People, Right Plan*. In it he tells us that we have inside information on God's will for our lives! He says that God has bestowed an incredible gift with every believer. He has given us an internal compass to guide and discern things about our lives, our families, our children, our finances, and much more.

Looking back I see now why I had peace about moving away from my family, friends, and my church body where I was so involved. God surely had a new *Right Place, Right People, and Right Plan* for my life.

I fell in love with the south my first visit shorty after Jesse's funeral. My cousin Debbie invited me to her beautiful vacation home there just one block from the beach. The beach has always been my favorite place to feel peaceful and relaxed, and now I think of it as a place that I can quiet my heart and have the Lord speak to me. It is the place that as I look out to the horizon and see no end, I'm reminded that that is just how God's love is for us…never ending! His love is deep and wide, and just as the waves wash in and out, so His grace keeps washing over us.

I asked Debbie's realtor friend Darlene about a possible small place I could look into buying to spend my summers. She told us of a spot to check out on our way to the airport at the end of that visit. It was an old cotton plantation that had the most beautiful entrance. It had a long narrow dirt road that appeared as if you were going into a different dimension. As you drove down the beautiful road of oak trees adorned with Spanish moss arched like a canopy, you could not help but feel like it was a special place. There was a small cottage coming up for sale that I looked at. I still get the chills thinking about how it was almost an audible voice that I heard as I stood on that property. The Lord told me that this would be my place of peace and restoration. I had this response: *What are you talking about, Lord? I'm doing better. You are helping me to recover from this deep pit of grief with all the love, support, and mentoring I'm getting.* It wasn't long after that that my husband of twenty-six years left me, not being able to handle his grief and looking for pain relief in all the wrong places. So this home started to really seem like a place that was my future. The day it came on the market there were four other people who had put in offers, yet I got the house.

I told Darlene that things had changed in my life, and I really needed to rent it. I knew I couldn't afford it with my husband gone and with Sami still in high school, so moving in the house then was out of the question. Darlene took care of looking for a possible tenant and eventually managed the property for me. She was so kind and soon became a dear friend. She invited me to stay at her home anytime I wanted to visit.

My mom got diagnosed with lung cancer shortly after I was going through my divorce. It was a trying time again. I was still numb and just going through the daily motions of life the best I knew how, staying in God's Word. You see my dad had also died unexpectedly just forty days before Jesse. He suffered with emphysema and COPD. I tried to just shelf that pain since, at that time, I had just been told by the doctors that Jesse had only weeks to live. My dad died peacefully in his lazy boy chair during the night. I believe that he just didn't want to see his grandchild go before him. I like picturing him in heaven greeting Jesse as he arrived so shortly after. My pastor told me that there is significance in the Bible of forty days. It led me to research this and soak in the riches of His Word.

The relief I was starting to feel knowing that Jesse didn't have to suffer any more quickly turned into dread again in seeing my mother go through her cancer treatment. How was I going to handle this? I would say to the Lord, *First my dad, then my son, and now my marriage—isn't that enough? I need my mom.* I remember feeling like I could not do this again—go into a hospital and watch another person I love deal with the horrors of cancer. I thanked God for my siblings who were there for her and me. Even going through radiation and pain, my mom's first concern was always for me, and she never complained. I thank God it was not a long time of suffering for her. My mom was my rock, and I was going to really miss her.

My sisters and I took a trip back to my cousin Debbie's house shortly after Mom's funeral. I got to show them my little place that was now rented, much to Darlene's surprise. Darlene had said to me, "I'm not sure how you are going to be able to rent this when there are over one hundred and seventy properties for rent right now, and no one really wants to be this far out of town." I told her, "Don't worry, it will rent because I know that God is preserving that house for me." I asked my daughter Sami to pray about going to college in the south so we could both move down there. My son Matt was now in the military. Even though I was supposed to sell the house in New York as part of the divorce agreement, the Lord kept us there until the month of Sami's high school graduation! I was so happy for her. My children had gone through enough, and I did not want to take her from her home and friends. She did get accepted into USC in Columbia, South Carolina, and I finally got to move into that sweet little cottage. Darlene was the only person I knew in South Carolina when I moved. My cousin had since sold her house. Darlene was so helpful with getting me accustomed to the southern ways. She told me I needed to talk slower and lower, be patient with workers, and I would do fine. I felt her compassion as she had experienced a real scare almost losing her husband Scott to cancer just a few years prior. I know she will hate to read this, but I felt she was like a mother, always looking out for me. The first thing Darlene said when I returned was, "You know, I want you to know that I believe you now that God preserved the house for you. It could've only been Him to have kept that rented these four years." I replied, "I'm so glad you believe that it was true."

> I pray that out of his glorious riches he may strengthen you with power through his Spirit in your inner being, so that Christ may dwell in your hearts through faith. And I pray that you, being rooted and established in love, may have power, together with all the Lord's holy people, to grasp how wide and long and high and deep is the love of Christ.
>
> —EPHESIANS 3:16–18, NIV

> For our light and momentary troubles are achieving for us an eternal glory that far outweighs them all.
>
> —2 CORINTHIANS 4:17, NIV

> In all this you greatly rejoice, though now for a little while you may have had to suffer grief in all kinds of trials.
>
> —1 PETER 1:6, NIV

Father God,

Thank you for the trials in my life. I never thought when I was in them that I would be thanking you for them. Yes, I thanked you for being there with me, but at the time I still would have preferred you not allow them. I can now say with a new heart that you refined me, you built character in me, you brought me to the realization of my complete, utter dependence on you even when circumstances are good. I can now say that as I continually surrender my life, you continually bless me and shower me with your love. Thank you. I love you. In the name of Jesus, Amen.

THE CENTER OF GOD'S WILL

I wanted to be sure I was in the will of God and living where He wanted me to be. I loved the south. I was glad I was only two hours away from Sami's college and enjoyed being so close to the beach.

One Sunday evening, I went back to church to view a DVD series being shown there. My heart filled with such joy because the Lord knew I had wanted to complete that series. I was studying the same one back in New York. Now here it was for me on a screen 800 miles away.

My friend Sue had told me that she knew a woman from her business that was also moving to South Carolina. Sue's son and Jesse were born a month apart and we were raising them as neighbors. When Jesse got sick she withdrew from our friendship. I understood knowing first hand that it's difficult for many people to deal with. The Lord had been working in Sue's life and she called me and apologized. I told her it was all right; I understood how close to home it was. When the Lord is in a friendship the bond as "sisters" keeps that friendship strong no matter how often you see the person, you can pick up where you left off. Sue and her husband rallied to help with the enormous crowds that gathered to honor Jesse at his funeral service at church. They set up a video so that the overflow could hear the service. They are a blessing to me and I'm thrilled to have them in my life. Sue gave me her friend Giovanna's phone number when I moved south and we connected. A series of events began to unwind; in retrospect, I saw how the Lord was going before me and making my transition flow smoothly. The day my moving truck came, Giovanna drove over and helped me unpack. I began to tell her how God was working in my life, and she thanked me, saying it was a reminder to her that she should get back to attending church.

One of the schools I was assigned to for my job led me to meet a high school teacher who was also a youth pastor. He had recently moved from Texas. He was attending the same church of a pastor that I had emailed seven months prior. A mutual pastor friend told me it would be a good church for me to attend if it weren't too far from my home. It was directly across from Giovanna's house, and so we visited there often. I had emailed that pastor and asked for three prayer requests. The Lord answered all of them. First was that Sami would be accepted at USC; second was that I would get a job; and third was that I would find a church home. The Lord was truly showing me He was guiding and directing me, yet I knew I still harbored a lot of hurt and anger I needed to address.

I called my friend Lisa who always had Godly wisdom. I had been upset with the realtor who sold my house and had promised to mail some money she owed me, yet she was not mailing the check. Lisa's advice was to ask the Lord to keep her up at night and convict her to do the right thing. That prayer was answered when only two days later the check arrived.

I called the online company that I had sold jewelry for asking if there were any representatives in my area, hoping to do that job part time again there. It wasn't long into the phone conversation that the woman rep that I called asked me if I was a Christian. She was a young mom named Amanda who was going through a terrible divorce. She really needed someone to share with. We got together, and I gave her some sermon tapes. She was very encouraged. Amanda started to attend church with me and saw the loving, spiritual family I had there. She also began to attend our small group study during the week as well. In that group she felt safe and allowed herself to be broken and vulnerable. She shared a secret that she had been keeping to herself which let the enemy keep her in bondage. She loved the Lord and wanted to be free of this. After a lot of prayer the Lord broke those chains that bound her and healed her heart. It was the beginning of another very good friendship.

Another Sunday after church I had trouble starting my daughter's car. Two nice men from the church came out to assist. Stu soon became a dear friend. He was an ex-marine who knew about cars. He later worked on the car in his free time and would not accept payment. I got to know him and his wife very well. They were the loving parents of three young girls. At this writing, it has only been a few months since Stu collapsed at his job as a firefighter and did not make it out of the hospital. He was thirty-one years old! I don't understand why him, such an amazing Christian man, yet I trust in the Lord. I grieve for his family. I know God will take care of them. I have peace that Stu is in glory! He is yet another example of how fragile life is, how we need to be prepared to meet our Creator. I know Stu was met by Jesus saying, "…Well done good and faithful servant…" (Matthew 25:23, NIV)!

The other gentleman named Rich had heard from the pastor that I did occupational therapy, and he referred me to the local hospital where he worked. I was hired for part-time work in their pediatric outpatient clinic after my school job. This enabled me to make enough money to get by. His wife Carrie and I were in Bible study together and became good friends.

The Lord was setting everything in place for me. These chains of events helped me to know that I was not alone; I was His child and He was taking good care of me. I knew that what the Lord whispered to me about this being a place of peace and restoration for me was truly happening. I was in the center of His will and there is no better place to be. I was in His favor and seeing His hand on all I was doing.

Time was passing so quickly, and I found myself thinking about my friend Debbie's brother Chip who I had met briefly at the church her husband pastors. Chip came to give blood and register for the bone marrow registry at a Jesse's Wish drive I held there. He wanted to honor Jesse's memory, knowing about him through Debbie. He had been praying for Jesse and me throughout Jesse's cancer. I had also been praying for him and his wife who was suffering with cancer at the same time and who also went home to be with the Lord. Our grief was our common bond, and the Lord used that to grow a special friendship through two years of e-mails before we ever saw one another again. I knew in my heart that the Lord had ordained our relationship. I was wishing time would go even faster so that I could see Chip soon. He was a gift from the Lord, and I just wanted to treasure God's every good and perfect gift. I can hear my friend Lisa saying that all I have to do is be right with the Lord and the rest will follow. I needed to train my mind that it wasn't about how much more I could *do* for the Lord. I knew I fell short. I just wanted to *be* more for Him. I was so thankful for His grace and His mercy and His blessings. I was actually starting to feel happy again. I knew God was slowing me down and had brought me to this new place to calm my anxious heart, hear from Him, listen to the waves, and remember that He walked on water! There is nothing too hard for Him! He asked me to step out in faith, and I did in obedience. I looked out at the horizon, and I knew that just as I didn't see an end, there was no end to the love that He has for us! I knew He was redeeming my life.

The profound grief was being lifted from my shoulders. Life was good again, and Chip was planning on finally visiting. My e-mail guy was becoming a tangible reality!

Christ has come that we might have life, and may have it abundantly.

—JOHN 10:10

For all have sinned and fall short of the glory of God.

—ROMANS 3:23, NIV

I will give you a new heart and put a new spirit within you; I will take the heart of stone out of your flesh and give you a heart of flesh. I will put My Spirit within you and cause you to walk in My statutes, and you will keep My judgments and do them. Then you shall dwell in the land that I gave to your fathers; you shall be My people, and I will be your God. I will deliver you from all your uncleanness. I will call for the grain and multiply it, and bring no famine upon you.

—EZEKIEL 36:26–29

Gracious Heavenly Father,

Thank you for bringing me to a place of peace and restoration. Thank you that your Word promises that, "Blessed are those who mourn for they shall be comforted." Thank you for those you bring into our lives even for a brief time. I look forward to meeting those who have died in Christ together in the clouds to ascend to our true home, heaven. In the name of Jesus, Amen.

DIVINE APPOINTMENTS

In August of 2010 I unpacked an old notebook in which I had listed all the positive things that were happening during Jesse's illness. Reading it again for the first time eight years later, not just feeling like such a different person but knowing that I was, helped me realize the shift in my perspective and contributed to my continued healing. Living in a place of new beginnings, I was now perceptively more aware that there are no coincidences, that all positive things are His blessings! I knew that the Lord was renewing my life. I was living in a beautiful place, attending a new church I loved, working at a new job, making new friends, and most importantly I had the time and opportunity to sit at His feet on the beach just a short walk from my little cottage. I was encouraged and excited for what He had in mind for me. I trusted in His promises that Liz had spoken over me. He had a plan for my life.

The Lord started confirming over and over that He was with me especially through the lonely days. I knew in my heart that I wanted to fall in love again and be married again, but if that was not His plan for me, it was okay. He was my bridegroom, and I depended on Him daily. I began to list all the ways that He was showing me

He was with me. I was not always consistent with my journaling but when something was on my heart that I felt so strongly about I would actually write it out to Him. I'm so glad I did that because, again, it shows me where I was, where I am, and how faithful He always is. I wrote to Jesus saying, "Who knows, someday, Lord, you may want me to write a book or write our story for my kids to read, or maybe just for me in my old age to remember." I laughed out loud and wrote, "I know you're laughing with me." Now my prayer is that these parts of my journals and stories of people He brought into our lives will show people how faithful God is, how He hears our prayers and answers them, though not always in our timing. Yes, He is a redeeming God!

It all began one bright sunny morning as I drove around investigating my new neighborhood in my new state of South Carolina. I saw a street named Daylily Drive. My mom's name was Lily, and so I smiled, turned down this quiet narrow street where the sign read "Daylilies for Sale." The mile-long narrow road led me to be warmly greeted by an elderly sweet woman named Mini. We had a nice conversation, and I soaked in all her knowledge of the beautiful flowers. As she rode her golf cart around and loaded my car with what I had purchased, she turned and hugged me. I instantly thought of my own mom and the love she so generously showed to everyone. I knew that was a big hug from the Lord and a precious memory of my sweet loving mom that I was missing so much. My second God-ordained moment was meeting Marissa. Marissa was a pretty nurse from Thailand. She also had a sign posted outside of her home that read, "Fruits and Vegetables for Sale." As I pulled down the driveway I could see that she had row after row of fig trees. She came out of the house to greet me, adorned with a big gold charm necklace that read, "Jesus loves me." She began to tell me what the Bible says about fig trees and said, "I have thirty of them, and they all belong to God." My reply was "Doesn't everything?" She gave me the high five sign. The next blessing was one that was so much more than a divine appointment; it was the Lord knowing exactly what I needed here in this quaint little town of Beaufort. I had a list of churches I wanted to visit when I got there, but one name not on the list was Seaside Vineyard Fellowship. I found out about it by pulling in the parking lot to look at a jeep for sale that my daughter wanted to see. That Sunday we went, and I knew that day it was where He wanted me. Pastor Mark and his wife Heidi welcomed us with open arms. I soon learned of his heart for the Lord, the humble way he served Him, and his willingness to be open and vulnerable to our church body. He has a heart for missions and puts himself in harm's way in one of the most dangerous parts of Africa to train up leaders and spread the gospel. On one of my first visits there I met a woman who was also single, a widow named Evelene. She soon became Queen Evelene as we often joked, and we shared many fun times together. It was as though God was not only giving me a Godly single woman to spend my time with, but also her parents, who became so dear to me that it felt like I had parents again! They would tell me how good I was for their daughter, and that she had a renewed spark for life hanging out with me. I argued, "No, she is good for me," and she was. I loved our time together on that beautiful island where her parents lived. We soon began to co-lead the women's Bible study, and the Lord used us to minister to one another as well as the other ladies in our group. We went to her parents' cabin in the mountains of Tennessee with some of the ladies from our study. We had an amazing time having church at the foot of an eighty-foot waterfall on the property. We placed a hiking stick in the water as we each grabbed hold of it speaking out scripture and declaring His promises for us. My friendship grew with Evelene, and I was thrilled with how God was using us to minister in the lady's Bible study. We shared the intimate details of our lives. She was happy for me when Chip finally came to visit. The three of us were sitting outdoors one night on the river, and I looked at her and said, "I know you won't mind because I'm going to go sit on his lap". She laughed and teased me about "my email guy," giving him the name "Chip-o-licious!"

> Think about the things of heaven, not the things of earth. For you died to this life, and your real life is hidden with Christ in God. And when Christ, who is your life, is revealed to the whole world, you will share in all his glory.
>
> —COLOSSIANS 3:2–4, NLT

Dear Lord,

Thank you for the dear friends you bring into our lives. You supply all of our needs. You take such good care of us. Your Word is the breath in our lungs. Thank you for using us to minister to others through your Word by the power of your Holy Spirit. Thank you for bringing people on our path who represent you and desire to worship you in spirit and truth. In the name of Jesus, Amen.

MARY AND MARCUS

Not only did the Lord arrange new people as friends in my life, He brought me family. That first Sunday at Seaside Fellowship a greeter gave me a card in case I wanted to sign up for any more information. I had checked off the small groups option and gave it back. Upon entering the church everyone was friendly, and I loved the sanctuary, which was an old movie theater. The worship band was on the stage, and as they began to praise Him, it was very evident that the Holy Spirit was there. Pastor Mark led worship and joked with me by saying "I'm sorry" when I told him I was from New York. He gave me a book on how the Vineyard churches began. His wife Heidi was very sweet and soon became a wonderful friend. I felt very much at peace there. After the first few worship songs they announced for us to go find someone to say hello to—somebody you don't know. So that obviously left me wide open, yet I felt in my spirit that I was supposed to go up to the interracial couple. I put out my hand and said my name and a big smile came across this tall, dark, handsome man's face as he showed me the card with my name on it that I had filled out from the greeter. He gently spoke, "I am Marcus and this is my wife

Mary." I took that nudging from the Holy Spirit to go up to them as a sign that the Lord was still arranging things and people to be in my life, and that He wanted me at that church. I looked forward to going the following week. The next day was my first day at my new job for the school district, and the orientation was in the high school for the thousands of employees. Who are the first two people I see in the hallway? Yes, Mary and Marcus! They were both teachers working for the same school district. That was the beginning of a friendship that quickly felt as though they had been my friends for most of my life. I had never felt more loved and accepted by new friends so quickly as I did with Mary and Marcus. I knew the Lord was making a way for me to not miss anyone or anything I left behind and that this was confirmation of where I was supposed to be. The next day while getting settled in my home, I hung up the print that my sisters gave me of Jesus in the boat calming the storm. I read the scripture on the bottom out loud before I walked out the door to go to Mary and Marcus's house for dinner and small group Bible study. When I got there Marcus began by saying that there had been a scripture on his heart all day. Yes, it was the same scripture I had just read on the print as I left my house. "He got up, rebuked the wind and said to the waves, 'Quiet! Be still!' Then the wind died down and it was completely calm" (Mark 4:39, NIV). This began the next part of my spiritual journey: to not only know the Word of the Lord even more, but to also use my authority to speak out His Word by the power of the Holy Spirit living in me. I yearned to be obedient to His call on my life. Mary and Marcus are perfect examples of how to live life that way. They have spent most of their lives doing exactly that, showing the love of Christ, giving of themselves selflessly to others. Prior to teaching they ran a boys home while raising their four beautiful children. I even got to love on and be loved by their grandchildren who soon began calling me "Mimi." Everywhere Mary and I went people thought we were sisters, and we both replied in unison the first time, "Yes, sisters in Christ!" We are so much alike—we love the same things and love doing the same things, and we were soon inseparable. Marcus was always generous to share his bride with me. I love that they were there when my romance with Chip first began to blossom. I kept telling her we were just email friends. He was never going to drive 700 miles to date me. Mary said she could tell from the expression on my face when Chip would call that he was the one for me. Well, of course she was right. He did come and my suspicions were right—we were more than just friends! After two years of exchanging emails, we already knew each other well. Chip was excited to meet Mary and Marcus, having heard so much about them from me. Marcus quickly befriended Chip and one day made him a little uncomfortable when he put his arm around him to pray as we walked through a parking lot back to our cars after a wonderful day kayaking together. I remember looking back at them and saying to Mary, "Oh no, this is not good," but it was good; it was something Chip needed in his life, a good Christian brother. Marcus became someone Chip looked up to and respected for his walk with the Lord. The four of us went on to have many good times together. Chip found a way for them to be included in our wedding day, as we were not inviting friends. He came up with the idea to have them be our photographers! I was thrilled! They were great at it as a hobby and did an amazing job for us, as well as blessing us with their presence. Although Chip and I have moved back up north for a while, no space or time can lessen the love and friendship we have with Mary and Marcus. We are joined by love for each other and most of all for the Lord. What brings us together while we are apart is prayer—being one in Spirit and Truth, lifting each other up, and knowing that miles may keep us apart, but we will be together for eternity in our true home, heaven.

Iron sharpens iron, and one man sharpens another.

—PROVERBS 27:17 ESV

Finally, all of you, have unity of mind, sympathy, brotherly love, a tender heart, and a humble mind.

—1 PETER 3:8, ESV

So then, while we have opportunity, let us do good to everyone, and especially to those who are of the household of faith.

—GALATIANS 6:10, ESV

For we are God's masterpiece. He has created usanew in Christ Jesus, so we can do the good things he planned for us long ago.

—EPHESIANS 2:10, NLT

Dear Lord,

Thank you for your faithful servants here on earth working for your kingdom. I pray that you would send all of us a brother or sister in Christ to walk with us on this journey. Thank you for your spirit of wisdom and discernment as we look to you for your guidance in our lives. In the name of Jesus, Amen.

Sweet Sherry

I was beyond excited when Chip decided to buy the house on the marsh after he asked me to marry him. It was such a gorgeous place. I just love the sprawling oak trees with the long pieces of Spanish moss hanging from them, gently blowing with the wind. We went back to the house at night to look at the view in the yard, sneaking down the side of the empty house laughing when we saw a man next door sitting in his chair near the window, not knowing we were there. Oh, the view was amazing! The Parris Island Bridge was lit in the background and the moon was reflecting on the high tide. I knew it was going to be another special place to call home, one I had only dreamed of ever living in with the love of my life!

The first neighbor that I met was a very pretty lady named Sherry. It seems everyone who doesn't hear a southern drawl will ask you where you are from. Sherry and I spoke of our roots and what had brought us to this beautiful place. In our first conversation she shared with me that she wanted the peace of this setting to help her overcome the grief of losing her twenty-year-old daughter to a horrific car accident. My heart just sank. What were the chances of living next door to another mom whose child passed away, and that it was only months apart from Jesse's death? My body began to tremble, as I knew the Lord had something special in mind for the both of us as friends. Sherry is a follower of Jesus Christ, which was just another awesome thing about her. You could see the peace and hope she possessed knowing she would see her daughter again. We laughed and cried together as we shared memories and pictures. She showed me a video made of the life of her beautiful daughter Kassandra. I must admit the thought that entered my mind. I wondered if it was worse to lose a child in such an unexpected, shocking way as a sudden tragic accident or to have years with them so ill and always knowing that they may die. Silly, I know. No scenario is better. They both stink; it just seems so unfair, so wrong that a mother buries her child. I found myself thinking about Mary, the mother of Jesus and just like God chose Mary, He chose me to be Jesse's mom and Sherry to be Kassandra's mom for a time and a purpose. Of course it was way too short a time, yet I believe we both would agree that these children were precious gifts to us, and it was far greater to have had them however brief. I think about what it must have been like for Mary, watching Jesus being beaten beyond recognition, carrying that heavy cross, nails being hammered into His hands and feet, hanging there until He died. I wonder if she was even aware then that His greatest burden was the separation from His Father as He carried the sins of the world—all of our sins, past, present and future—becoming the final sacrifice, the finished work, and giving us the victory to defeat sin.

The one thing we can all be sure of is death. The question is where will we spend eternity: heaven or hell? The Bible tells us Jesus answered, "I am the way and the truth and the life. No one comes to the Father except through me" (John 14:6, NIV).

Today we find many different avenues people walk through looking to fill that empty place, wondering what will be when they die. I believe our Creator made us with the spiritual yearning to seek those answers, and I believe He pursues us continually. We get to choose. He will not force His will on us. He has given us the simple gospel truth. We were all born sinners. Sin came into this world with Adam. We ask forgiveness, and the blood of Jesus Christ gives it to us. He came to set us free. We are saved by grace through faith; there is nothing we can do or not do to change that. Salvation is a free gift He gives us when we profess Him as our Lord and Savior.

We were all born in our mother's wombs, and we can all be born again in the Spirit. What will you choose? Today is the day of salvation. Today you can decide to have eternity in heaven, and the angels will rejoice when you confess with your mouth that Jesus is Lord and believe in your heart that God raised Him from the dead; you will be saved.

> For with the heart one believes and is justified, and with the mouth one confesses and is saved.
>
> —ROMANS 10:10, ESV

> Do not let your hearts be troubled. You believe in God; believe also in me. My Father's house has many rooms; if that were not so, would I have told you that I am going there to prepare a place for you?
>
> —JOHN 14:1–2, NIV

> Brothers and sisters, we do not want you to be uninformed about those who sleep in death, so that you do not grieve like the rest of mankind, who have no hope. For we believe that Jesus died and rose again, and so we believe that God will bring with Jesus those who have fallen asleep in him. According to the Lord's word, we tell you that we who are still alive, who are left until the coming of the Lord, will certainly not precede those who

have fallen asleep. For the Lord himself will come down from heaven, with a loud command, with the voice of the archangel and with the trumpet call of God, and the dead in Christ will rise first. After that, we who are still alive and are left will be caught up together with them in the clouds to meet the Lord in the air. And so we will be with the Lord forever. Therefore encourage each other with these words.

—1 THESSALONIANS 4:13–18, NIV

There is a time for everything, and a season for every activity under the heavens: a time to be born and a time to die, a time to plant and a time to uproot, a time to kill and a time to heal, a time to tear down and a time to build, a time to weep and a time to laugh, a time to mourn and a time to dance.

—ECCLESIASTES 3:1–4, NIV

Lord,

Thank you for the gift of faith. Thank you that your Word says we only need the faith of a mustard seed, and we can move mountains. Thank you for bringing friends alongside us so we can encourage and comfort each other with the truth of your Word and the hope that we have in you. In the name of Jesus, Amen.

SWEET GEORGIE OF MINE

Wow! Can it be thirty-six years? That's a lasting friendship! I can still see her pretty young face carrying her four-month-old child the first time we met. Now all these years later she's still as pretty, still as sweet, still as loving, only now we are not just friends but sisters in Christ. We instantly became friends, which was a good thing since our husbands were best friends. I did think she was a little prudish at the time because I was so in the world, and she was beginning to hear about our true citizenship, our true identity, and our true treasures. It was fun being young moms together. For a while it was her two girls and my two boys, although Matt didn't come along for six more years after her first child Joy. When Jesse was born five years later my husband and I really wanted Georgie and her husband to be Jesse's Godparents. I love looking back and seeing how God so amazingly arranges things for our good even when we don't know Him. We enjoyed each other's homes and extended families, always together cooking up the usual big Italian feasts. Georgie loves to cook and is very good at it. She sparked my interest in it and between her and my mom, I began to acquire quite a collection of recipes. She also began to spark my interest in Jesus. Looking back, it was

Him in her that was so attractive to me. Friends of theirs would come to their home with a Bible and begin to reveal to us the things that were exciting them. I guess the world and my life we're just too busy at the time for me to respond to the call God always had on my life. I thank Him and praise Him that our friendship grew and remained strong, and we were always there for each other. We are both no longer married to the men that brought us together, but we are both very grateful to them for that. I love how the Lord used her to ask me to join her at the Christian church near my mom's house, which she would join me in visiting afterward. Those were special Sundays for us. Though I know Georgie loved and loves all my children, having been Jesse's Godmother, he was very special to her. It was more than special to me to have her there with me throughout his illness and on her knees at his bedside the day he went home to the Lord. I am truly blessed with a strong loyal friend. I'm glad to be at a time in our lives where we can just laugh a lot after so many tears. It was more than an honor for me to have her stand at my side as my maid of honor at my wedding three years ago and to now share tears of joy together seeing how God is redeeming our lives!

Yet some things have changed. Conversations about our children are different now. We know to trust them to the Lord as we practice the power of prayer together and see His continued hand on all our lives.

> My command is this: Love each other as I have loved you. Greater love has no one than this: to lay down one's life for one's friends.
>
> —JOHN 15:12–13, NIV

> Therefore, confess your sins to one another and pray for one another, that you may be healed. The

prayer of a righteous person has great power as it is working.

—JAMES 5:16, ESV

Likewise the Spirit helps us in our weakness. For we do not know what to pray for as we ought, but the Spirit himself intercedes for us with groanings too deep for words.

—ROMANS 8:26, ESV

Call to me and I will answer you, and will tell you great and hidden things that you have not known.

—JEREMIAH 33:3, ESV

And another angel came and stood at the altar with a golden censer, and he was given much incense to offer with the prayers of all the saints on the golden altar before the throne, and the smoke of the incense, with the prayers of the saints, rose before God from the hand of the angel. Then the angel took the censer and filled it with fire from the altar and threw it on the earth, and there were peals of thunder, rumblings, flashes of lightning, and an earthquake.

—REVELATION 8:3–5, ESV

Lord Jesus,

Thank you for the privilege of prayer. Thank you that you make our requests known to the Father. Thank you that you keep our prayers in the bowls of heaven and in your perfect timing you mix them with your fire and pour them back down to earth to change our situation and answer our prayers! Help us to linger in our prayers and wait patiently for you. In the name of Jesus, Amen.

GEORGIE AND JESSE

A CHILDLIKE JOY

How good is our God that He is always speaking to us, pursuing us, and with us even when we are not aware of it. He desires so much to have relationship with us and to speak to us. I love having dreams that I know are from Him. One very special dream occurred during the time that I was doing a Bible study with a book called *One Thousand Gifts*, which focused on being thankful for everything and having a heart of gratitude. He gave me a peace with the notion that if I was going to be a single woman for the rest of my life, that would be okay because I had my bridegroom Jesus. I was very grateful that the Lord brought Chip into my life. God had brought me to a place of restoration, alone and away from familiar people, things, and places. It was then that the Lord gave me my heart's desire, bringing such a Godly man as Chip into my life.

I had been thinking, *what are the chances for us when we live so far apart?* Well, my email guy did finally drive the 700 miles after two work related postponements in search of a retirement home for *himself*, so he thought. It was so much fun looking for homes for him and hearing him ask me what I thought about this kitchen or that kitchen. Fast-forward three more visits, a canceled fishing trip day, his day on the beach with the Lord, a marriage proposal, and a house offer. We now reside part-time in this beautiful home on the water as I'm reminded daily of God's hand on our lives. He gave us this place to reflect on His amazing creation and all that He has done to restore our lives.

When Chip visited in December of 2012 it was the fourth trip he had made to see me again when I saw myself in a dream as a child, dancing and holding hands with other children in a circle. I was filled with so much joy in my heart. A few days later Chip asked me to marry him, to my surprise, yet I knew almost from the beginning that I loved this man, and he was a gift from our Father.

On New Year's Day we worshiped together in church. I looked up and on the screen, as the background of a new song called "Furious," there were children in a circle dancing and laughing exactly as I had seen in my dream! I praised the Lord, with tears streaming down my face, for this confirmation that He had brought this wonderful man to me, and that He was putting joy back into my heart again after years of grieving. This dream led to the marriage vows I wrote to my husband on that special day that we became one.

FURIOUS: BY JEREMY RIDDLE

Nothing can tear us from
The grip of His mighty love
We've only glimpsed, His vast affection
Heard whispers of, His heart and passion
It's pouring out…
His love is deep, His love is wide
And it covers us
His love is fierce, His love is strong
It is furious

His love is sweet, His love is wild
And it's waking hearts to life
The Father loves and sends His son
The Son lays down His life for all
He lavishes His love upon us
He calls us now, His sons and daughters
He's reaching out…
…and its waking hearts to life
He is waking hearts to life.

OUR WEDDING VOWS

Chip,

Loving you has enabled me to receive more of God's love. I have always known that He was here with me, holding my hand, putting His arm around me, giving me His shoulder on which to rest my weary head, wiping my tears away with His hand, embracing my face…just loving me! Now I know that He is lifting me up like a child and spinning me around, and I can't stop smiling. This newfound innocence, sense of wonder and joy He has given me in giving me you to love. You are a precious gift from our Father and a wonderful reflection of His love. I will love and share with you all this life has to offer with Jesus in the center of that love. I will honor you and be faithful to you all the days of our lives as we praise Him and thank Him together as one.

Marian,

I thank God for giving us a second chance at happiness. I love you and know that this love is from God. I thank the Lord for the love that has brought our hearts and lives together. Through all the uncertainties and trials of the present and future, I promise to stay by your side. I promise to work at our love and always make you a priority in my life. I promise to love you without reservation, comfort you in times of trials, encourage you to achieve all your goals and dreams, laugh with you, cry with you, grow with you spiritually, and always be open and honest with you. With every breath that God gives me and every beat of my heart I will love you. This is my promise to you.

While praying about our wedding vows we meditated on the scripture in Ecclesiastes 4 that a three-strand cord is not easily broken. Just as a wedding band (a continuous circle) is a symbol of never-ending love, we wanted a symbol of the three cords—Chip and I with Jesus at the center. This led us to look for matching wedding bands with three colors of gold—white, yellow, and rose—braided together representing that scripture. We acknowledged that we were entering into an important covenant that God ordained. I encourage you to look into the scriptures on covenants; the old covenant God made with Abraham and the new covenant between God and Jesus. You will see the value God places on them as well as in the covenant of marriage. His Word is a lamp for our feet and a light on our path (Psalm 119:105, NIV).

Sadly, our world today does not value that covenant any longer and families are suffering as a result. One purpose of a covenant is to get rid of weakness. A man and wife joined in the covenant of marriage balance out each other, build each other up. Chip and I experience that in our marriage making the effort to live out our vows and to grow even closer to one another and to God. We see His blessings in our marriage as a result of our obedience to His Word and we hope and pray that we will be an encouragement to others.

> As iron sharpens iron, so one person sharpens another.
>
> —PROVERBS 27:17, NIV

> In your anger do not sin": Do not let the sun go down while you are still angry.
>
> —EPHESIANS 4:26, NIV

> Do not let any unwholesome talk come out of your mouths, but only what is helpful for building others up according to their needs, that it may benefit those who listen.
>
> —EPHESIANS 4:29, NIV

> Two people are better off than one, for they can help each other succeed.
>
> —ECCLESIASTES 4:9, NLT

> The Spirit of the Lord God is upon me, because the Lord has anointed me to bring good news to the poor; he has sent me to bind up the brokenhearted, to proclaim liberty to the captives, and the opening of the prison to those who are bound; to proclaim the year of the Lord's favor, and the day of vengeance of our God; to comfort all who mourn; to grant to those who mourn in Zion—to give

them a beautiful headdress instead of ashes, the oil of gladness instead of mourning, the garment of praise instead of a faint spirit; that they may be called oaks of righteousness, the planting of the Lord, that he may be glorified. They shall build up the ancient ruins; they shall raise up the former devastations; they shall repair the ruined cities, the devastations of many generations.

—ISAIAH 61:1–4, ESV

Dear Lord,

Thank you for creating us with a longing to worship you from our innermost beings. Thank you for loving us. Thank you for confirming your will for our lives through your Word, through people, and through worship music. I long for the day I will sing praise to you unceasingly, for you are worthy to be praised! Thank you for your favor on our lives and your strength to live out the task you have planned for us. In the name of Jesus, Amen.

CHIP

Recently I have been thinking about Ruth, the great-granddaughter of Lot. We're told to remember Lot's wife who turned back to look at the sin in the land of Sodom and became a pillar of salt. Our merciful God sent angels to lead them out of the city before He destroyed it. Where is God leading you today? Don't look back! Ruth, the great-granddaughter of Lot was a cursed Moabite, and God used her in the genealogy of our precious Jesus! When my friend Lisa was praying for my marriage, she said the Lord reminded her of Ruth and that Chip is my Boaz. All I need to do is be right with the Lord, and everything will go fine. There were many days I'd hear the enemy whisper to me that I did not deserve a man as humble, generous, loving, kind, and as funny as Chip. I know Satan is a liar and a thief, so I chose not to listen. In my spirit I knew that God loved me more than I could fathom and just because my first marriage did not work out, didn't mean that God's plan wasn't to give me my heart's desire. Yes, He has given me my Boaz, and there is more to glean than I can even carry! I especially love the story of Ruth because it happened during one of the greatest famines. Those three years of watching my son fight that cancer was hopefully the greatest famine of my life, and if it was not, I know He will always give me the strength to endure. He has given me someone to love and be loved by, to go through any trials together as one, united in marriage. I did not always grasp the truth in God's Word that when two people join in the covenant of marriage, they become "one." My marriage to Chip is teaching me that with Jesus at the center of a marriage, as the third strand, the cord is so strong it cannot be broken.

"And though a man might prevail against one who is alone, two will withstand him—a threefold cord is not quickly broken" (Ecclesiastes 4: 12, ESV).

I know my husband would want me to share his experience on the rooftop of my home his very first visit to me in South Carolina. He has since admitted how he didn't want to drive his spotless Camaro over the sandy graveled road into the plantation where my house was. The first thing he noticed was how many leaves were stuck in the gutters of my roof. He came back from Lowe's with a leaf blower as my housewarming gift. I thought it was a very nice gesture, however, not very romantic. I just wanted to get to the beach with him, but somehow I knew he was going up on that roof first. When he finally came down I noticed that his eyes were very red, and I assumed that he had gotten dust in them, only to find out I was wrong. He had been overwhelmed to the point of tears. He revealed to me that he had a close relationship with the Lord, but he had never had the supernatural experience that he had just encountered on my roof. It was very clear and very plain to him that the Lord was thanking him for doing this kind act for Jesse's mom. He said the presence of the Lord was so powerful that he did not want to come down from the roof. He wanted to know all that there was to know about this young man, my son. We spent the next few hours on beautiful Hunting Island Beach sharing my memories of my precious child. Then we just sat quietly reading and enjoying God's amazing creation that surrounded us. The day evolved into a very romantic dinner at a small table overlooking the beautiful Beaufort River. He began to share the intimate details of the loss of his loving wife whom he shared life with for nearly thirty years.

He said a weight had been lifted off his shoulders by giving the intimate details of that story for the first time. I knew I could really love this man just hearing the capacity of love his heart contained. He kept apologizing for unloading like that, not wanting it to be a sad, serious evening; however, I was very grateful that he felt comfortable enough to share that story. It was just the beginning of what would be many intimate conversations.

Well, we all know that every fairytale has a wicked character, and no doubt the enemy made his way into this God-ordained relationship. A lot of prayer and complete, open, honest, conversations got us through the few rough patches. It was probably almost a year before I realized how much marrying me so quickly was out of his personality and character. I just love him even more knowing He was obedient to the Lord's revelation to him rather than doing what would have been his "normal' way of approaching any serious decision.

So, Satan did not like that obedience to God and started attacking. I was blessed to have a lot of good teachings about spiritual warfare under the mentorship of Pastor Mike and Lisa. I'm surely not saying that I'm immune to the lies of the enemy; I think I just recognize them a bit sooner now and know how to resist believing those lies. My husband, however, was not used to spiritual warfare. He would say, "I've been a middle-of-the-road Christian most of my life and since the Lord brought us together I've begun feeling attacked." I got really scared that he would take the easy way out and not want to deal with the warfare in order to be used as a couple by the Lord. How happy I am that I was wrong. His walk in obedience, his love for the Lord, is so strong that he recognized those lies and overcame them as we prayed and prayed through them. It is a battle; it requires a good fight. I'd like to forget that night when he came back south and wanted to talk about why I was the one to initiate my divorce. He struggled with the fact that the divorce could have kept my husband from coming to know the Lord. I needed to explain to him that it was not something I took or did lightly, that I prayed and I asked the Lord to give me direction. I also counseled with my pastor. My heart told me that because of his adultery and abandonment, I was released from the covenant of marriage. The day I needed to make a decision to call an attorney, I was seeking the Lord. There was no way that I could even go to speak to this attorney without twenty-five hundred dollars. Within that same week I received a check in the mail that was a refund from medical insurance for overpayment of the covered percentage. The check was for twenty-five hundred dollars!

I tried to let my fiancé know that I understood that God hates divorce, but sometimes there are no other options. The last thing I wanted to do was to bring more pain into my children's lives after losing their sibling by splitting up our family, yet I knew I needed to move forward in the call that the Lord had for my life. I wanted to understand His purpose—how a loving God could say "no" to our prayers, yet we continue to trust that He loves us.

The conversation that night was hard but necessary. With what felt like my heart breaking all over again, I took the ring off and gave it back with much hesitation and fear that my dream was already ending. I feared more heartache in my life. It was hard for both of us knowing that we would have adjustments and a past to move forward from. We had both been alone for six years and had finally come to a place where we were okay with the lives we had. Is *just okay* enough when you can share the love we knew we had for each other, a love poured out from our heavenly Father that would flow through us. We had no doubt that God brought us together and that He had a plan for us. We made a decision to move forward with our marriage plans and continued to bathe ourselves in prayer. We knew we could trust that God does not make mistakes. He has shown us His faithfulness. Looking back now I realize that this is what the Lord used to teach us how to really press forward in prayer together and confront areas in our lives that still needed His healing. We speak aloud the promises of God knowing the Word of God has power and never comes back void. We continue to grow closer together in Him and to each other. We have an amazing marriage, and I am grateful every day for Chip. Our strengths and weaknesses balance out each other. I never imagined marriage could be so fulfilling.

OUR WEDDING VERSE:

But just as it is written [in Scripture], "Things which the eye has not seen and the ear has not heard, And which have not entered the heart of man, All that God has prepared for those who love Him [who hold Him in affectionate reverence, who obey Him, and who gratefully recognize the benefits that He has bestowed]."

— 1 CORINTHIANS 2:9, AMP

But the Lord is faithful, and he will strengthen you and protect you from the evil one.

— 2 THESSALONIANS 3:3, NIV

Behold, I give you the authority to trample on serpents and scorpions, and over all the power of the enemy, and nothing shall by any means hurt you.

—LUKE 10:19

The weapons we fight with are not the weapons of the world. On the contrary, they have divine power to demolish strongholds. We demolish arguments and every pretension that sets itself up against the knowledge of God, and we take captive every thought to make it obedient to Christ.

—2 CORINTHIANS 10:4–5

Trust in the Lord with all your heart; do not depend on your own understanding. Seek his will in all you do, and he will show you which path to take.

—PROVERBS 3:5–6, NLT

Heavenly Father,

I could never thank you enough for the beautiful covenant of marriage. I pray, Lord, for this covenant today that seems to have become almost irrelevant in this world. I pray for those who are married that you would strengthen their union, that you would remind them to put their focus on you. Thank you that we have the victory over the enemy in our lives. In the name of Jesus, Amen.

THE PURSE

I could hardly contain the joy in my heart and excitement over our upcoming wedding. Being in my fifties didn't take away from the desire for the special day to be perfect. We were so happy and so anxious to see God's plan for our lives together. I knew I needed to pray and ask the Lord to give me His peace since I was struggling with feeling like I was being compared to his late wife knowing how much he loved her. God is so good! Right after that prayer I decided to watch a movie called "Safe Haven." The storyline was that of a young man, who was also a widower, with two children who meets a young woman he falls in love with. No, I did not know the synopsis before I put the movie on. The character in the movie struggled with the uncomfortableness of being with another woman almost as though he was being unfaithful. He finds out that his late wife had left him some letters, and he reads one in which she gave her blessing for him to be happy. She wanted him to be in love again and to get married again. Now I am sobbing my eyes out on the couch with the dog looking at me like I'm crazy. I knew in my spirit that it was the Lord who arranged this movie for me to see. Yes, He can even use movies to speak to us. Chip and I were in the process of packing things up because the beautiful home he built for her is now about to sell. He tried several times for a few years to sell the home, and it just wasn't the Lord's timing. I know it was hard for his girls to see me take things down and stage the house to show possible buyers. I know it was a very hard time for him too, yet he was gracious enough to know that I needed to feel like it was my home, to put my touch on it until it sold and we moved to a home of our own. Earlier that same evening while unpacking some things in the guestroom closet, I saw a Coach purse. My first thought was *I don't even remember buying this purse*. I opened it up to find that it was his late wife's. I looked in her wallet and saw pictures of their girls when they were young, their young nephews that I now know as young adults, money, and even her lipstick color! It felt so surreal. It was as though she had just left the house with her purse at home, yet almost eight years had passed. I started trembling as he walked past the room, realized what had just happened, and took it from my hand feeling a little embarrassed that I had found it. He told me that he didn't even remember that he had placed it in there. I asked the Lord, "Why this tonight after I just prayed for you to help me have peace about her?" I didn't see then how God had used that purse to bring about a major change in me. She became so real to me after looking in her purse that I felt as though I had met her. That very night I saw her in my dream. She touched my face and said simply, "Smile." That dream was such a blessing! It was such a release for me to love this man, even more so to receive his love. I somehow knew that she was happy for us and that she wanted to bless our marriage. Her dad has since introduced me as "his other daughter." The Lord gave me the peace that I had asked Him for. Chip and I are so blessed as our lives have multiplied with each other's new family relationships.

I have always wondered why the Bible says there is no marriage in heaven. I'm beginning to see now, after experiencing more of God's love, and the love of this man, that no matter how great a love we experience in a relationship, even in the covenant of marriage, it can't compare to the relationship and covenant that we have with the Lord.

And he said, "Hear my words: If there is a prophet among you, I the Lord make myself known to him in a vision; I speak with him in a dream."

—NUMBERS 12:6, ESV

In peace I will both lie down and sleep; for you alone, O LORD, make me dwell in safety.

—PSALM 4:8, ESV

For in the resurrection they neither marry nor are given in marriage, but are like angels in heaven.

—MATTHEW 22:30, ESV

Gracious Heavenly Father,

Thank you for the peace you give us, which transcends all understanding and guards our hearts and minds in Christ Jesus. Thank you for all the ways and times you pursue us and speak to us. Thank you for multiplying our lives in ways we never even imagined for ourselves. In the name of Jesus, Amen.

My Marine Kellie

There are so many songs I find solace in, just listening to the words and worshiping the Lord through them. One particular song called "Homesick" by Mercy Me really touched my heart. I put it on the website that I created for "Jesse's Wish."

Homesick

You're in a better place, I've heard a thousand times
And at least a thousand times I've rejoiced for you
But the reason why I'm broken, the reason why I cry
Is how long must I wait to be with you

I close my eyes and I see your face
If home's where my heart is then I'm out of place
Lord, won't you give me strength to make it through somehow
I've never been more homesick than now

Help me Lord cause I don't understand your ways
The reason why I wonder if I'll ever know
But, even if you showed me, the hurt would be the same
Cause I'm still here so far away from home

I close my eyes and I see your face
If home's where my heart is then I'm out of place
Lord, won't you give me strength to make it through somehow
I've never been more homesick than now

In Christ, there are no goodbyes
And in Christ, there is no end
So I'll hold onto Jesus with all that I have
To see you again
To see you again

And I close my eyes and I see your face
If home's where my heart is then I'm out of place
Lord, won't you give me strength to make it through somehow
Won't you give me strength to make it through somehow
Won't you give me strength to make it through somehow
I've never been more homesick than now.

Well, He did give me the strength to make it through somehow. One of those people He brought into my life through this song is a young Marine named Kellie serving in Iraq. She was missing being home so much that she googled this song, and it linked her to Jesse's website. She emailed me such a beautiful, compassionate letter, and I naturally responded to her. It started like this: "After I was able to stop crying long enough to see my computer screen, I felt led to reach out to you." In what can only be described as a divine appointment for us to comfort each other, our lives touched." We talked about our fight, so different yet so much the same. As Christians we know that this is not our true home. Fear, grief, and loneliness are still very real emotions that I am sure we were both facing. We talked about the fact that we don't know how people who don't know the Lord ever get past those things. That email was eleven years ago now, and we have never yet met in person. We keep in touch mostly through Facebook as I see her sweet life unfold. She's a wonderful young Christian woman and a worship leader in her church. We enjoy talking about the same music that we both love to worship to. She has a young son and just gave birth to a beautiful baby girl right before building their new home. I called her recently to tell her how happy I was for her, how I think about her almost every morning because I can faintly hear the sound of freedom as the Marines practice shooting at Parris Island. Kellie was from the south and still misses it. She knows that she will always be welcome in our home. I pray we do meet in person someday before we meet in heaven.

> Fear not, for I am with you; be not dismayed, for I am your God; I will strengthen you, I will help you, I will uphold you with my righteous right hand.
>
> —ISAIAH 41:10, ESV

> No man shall be able to stand before you all the days of your life. Just as I was with Moses, so I will be with you. I will not leave you or forsake you.
>
> —JOSHUA 1:5, ESV

> Even though I walk through the valley of the shadow of death, I will fear no evil, for you are with me; your rod and your staff, they comfort me.
>
> —PSALM 23:4, ESV

> For here we do not have an enduring city, but we are looking for the city that is to come.
>
> —HEBREWS 13:14, NIV

Dear God,

Thank you for our military. Thank you for these selfless souls who fight for our freedom. Thank you that you have placed believers in these dark places of war to bring hope to those around them, trusting in your sovereignty and protection. Thank you for bringing them home safely and blessing them with family. I pray protection over their minds and healing to their injured bodies. In the name of Jesus, Amen.

DALE

God brings us just the right person to come alongside us at just the right time. Dale had already been going to Risen King when Jesse went home to be with the Lord. I didn't really know her then. She was the pretty, young, shy woman who I had seen and later found out had been the one to volunteer to set up the meal at the church on Jesse's funeral day. Shortly after the funeral I began to experience some physical ailments, one in particular was a herniated disc that was terribly painful. I went to my doctor, and to my surprise, the nurse practitioner was Dale. She was very loving and compassionate. We became close friends very fast, sitting with each other every week at church and joining the Bible studies that were offered together. We especially shared the love of worship music. I suggested we go to a Christian concert and that was it, she was hooked. It became something we looked forward to doing together often.

We decided one weekend to fly to Atlanta together for a College of Prayer conference. It was a very powerful time of prayer, teaching, and healing. The pastor had us share a little bit on the first evening, which led to one of the youth pastors approaching me the next morning before the session began. He said the little I shared about losing both my parents, my son, and my twenty-six-year marriage all within three years led the Lord to give him a vision about me.

He said he saw the higher echelon of angels surrounding me and praying. They said, like Job who suffered many losses one after the other, the Lord was pleased that I remained faithful to him. He could see many blessings coming into my life for persevering through these trials. He prayed for me as the second session of the conference was just beginning. The Lord sent His Holy Spirit to work in Dale's heart that night. The topic was forgiveness. Dale knew that she had not forgiven her ex-husband for the abuse in their marriage. She was even unable to utter his name. For thirteen years she had referred to him as "the girls' father." It was time for that stumbling block to be broken. She began to weep and knew that that chain was being broken. Shortly after this time he developed cancer, and Dale was able to care for him, love on him, pray over him and bring him to know the Lord.

We use the word *miracle* lightly when something good happens from something bad, but Dale knew that this was a miracle in her life. His cancer was tremendously progressed, yet he remains cancer free today. The freedom she received allowed God to use her to bring many of her cancer patients that she cares for in her hospital to the Lord. After she went on a medical mission trip to Uganda, Africa, in 2009, she co-founded and developed a nonprofit organization in East Africa and the Caribbean.

That was only the beginning. Her foundation does so much more now, and she has seen the Lord complete healing in the lives of those who cry out to Him. In the second year that Dale and I were being discipled at our church, Pastor Mike encouraged us to co-lead a small group for one of his teaching series. We felt unequipped, but we knew that the Word told us that it was the Holy Spirit who would work through us and that we were just a vessel. It was an emotional healing course that Pastor Mike taught for the second time. So many lives were healed and changed through the first teaching in that church, especially mine. It's been such a blessing to have a sister in

Christ like Dale. Though we don't live in the same place anymore or attend church together, we know that we are one in spirit and in truth. We are so grateful to have been chosen to allow the Holy Spirit to speak to us and comfort us through the teaching of our pastor. It gave us the confidence to walk out the purpose and assignment that He had for us. Knowing our identity in Him and the authority we have from Him gave us the strength.

> For if you forgive other people when they sin against you, your heavenly Father will also forgive you. But if you do not forgive others their sins, your Father will not forgive your sins.
>
> —MATTHEW 6:14–15, NIV

> Bear with each other and forgive one another if any of you has a grievance against someone. Forgive as the Lord forgave you.
>
> —COLOSSIANS 3:13, NIV

> Get rid of all bitterness, rage and anger, brawling and slander, along with every form of malice. Be kind and compassionate to one another, forgiving each other, just as in Christ God forgave you.
>
> —EPHESIANS 4:31–32, NIV

> The angel said to him, "I am Gabriel! I stand in the presence of God, and I have been sent to speak to you and to tell you this good news."
>
> —LUKE 1:19, NIV

> Blessed the one who perseveres under trial because, having stood the test, that person will

receive the crown of life that the Lord has promised to those who love him.

—JAMES 1:12, NIV

Dear Lord,

Thank you for sending your Son as the perfect example of forgiveness. Thank you that because He forgave, we can forgive. Thank you for helping us to love the unlovable. Thank you for the freedom we receive when we forgive. Help us to call to our minds those we still need to forgive even when we think we already have. In the name of Jesus, Amen.

MARK SCHULTZ

Driving to and from New York City every day for treatment was a real challenge. The attacks of 9/11 were only five weeks after our daily trips into the city had begun. As mentioned before, we would have been there when the planes hit if it weren't for the hospital giving us Yankee tickets to the one o'clock game that day. That day was so surreal to me. Even though I watched it unfold on television I could not bring myself, after that day, to listen to one more report or see one more horrific scene. I can remember thinking it must be the end of the world. How much worse could life be? Our thirty-mile trip now took three hours. I would pray that Jesse would stay asleep and not get nauseous so that I would not have to pull off the highway. I looked forward to listening to Charles Stanley on the radio knowing that I needed to hear the Word of God to make it through the day. We could have stayed at the Ronald McDonald House, but we wanted to get home to be with family. We needed some sort of normalcy for a few hours before doing it all again. Worship music was also such a comfort to me for the journey. One particular evening I was listening to a Mark Schultz song that most of the moms from the hospital knew and would listen to as a prayer. It is called "He's My Son." I hung onto every lyric in that song as a way to pray when words failed me.

"He's My Son"

I'm down on my knees again tonight,
I'm hoping this prayer will turn out right.
See, there is a boy that needs Your help.
I've done all that I can do myself
His mother is tired,
I'm sure You can understand.
Each night as he sleeps
She goes in to hold his hand,
And she tries
Not to cry
As the tears fill her eyes.

Can You hear me?
Am I getting through tonight?
Can You see him?
Can You make him feel all right?
If You can hear me
Let me take his place somehow.
See, he's not just anyone, he's my son.

Sometimes late at night I watch him sleep,
I dream of the boy he'd like to be.
I try to be strong and see him through,
But God, who he needs right now is You.
Let him grow old,
Live life without this fear.
What would I be
Living without him here?
He's so tired,
And he's scared
Let him know that You're there.

As I wiped the tears from my eyes Jesse awoke and asked me to put on track fourteen. I was surprised that he knew what was on that track. Looking back now I realize that he had to have felt the presence of God in that car also! He wanted to lift up his own prayer through the song he liked on track fourteen: "I Am the Way:"

"I Am the Way"

You've got a secret no one knows
Locked away where no one goes
Deep inside your heart,
It's tearin' you apart.
You hide the pain in all you do,
Still the shackles binding you are heavier than stone,
But you are not alone.

When you're down
Look around
And you'll see I am with you.
Look to Me and you'll see I will be there to guide you.
Take My hand and I can lead you on for you know:

I am the answer,
And I am the way.
I am the promise,
And I have called your name.

So you want a brand new start
Askin' Me into your heart,
Down on bended knee
For the world to see.
And the chains around your heart
Fall away and break apart
Suddenly you see
The truth has set you free.

When you're down
Look around
And you'll see I am with you
Look to Me and you'll see I will be there to guide you
Take My hand and I can lead you on for you know:

I am the answer,
And I am the way.
I am the promise, and
I have called your name.

Surrounded by darkness

You stumbled along
Knowing the road that you traveled was long
But I'm here beside you,
Yes here all along,
The one that will carry you on.

When you're down
Look around
And you'll see I am with you.
Look to Me and you'll see I will be there to guide you.
Take My hand and I can lead you on for you know.

I am the answer,
And I am the way,
I am the promise and
I have called.

Oh when you are down
You think no one's around,
But I'll be with you both night and day.
I know the good times,
I'll see you through bad times,
Oh you know that I'm here to stay.

I am the answer,
And I am the way
I am the promise,
And I have called your name.

Jesse truly did call on the Lord for help that day. It wasn't long after that day that he gave his life to Christ with the encouragement of his tutor Liz.

I chose to have that song played at his funeral. In his eulogy I reminded everyone there that Jesse's strength was not of himself but from the Lord.

About a year after the funeral I had the opportunity to tell this story to the person on the phone as I was purchasing tickets to go see Mark Schulz with my daughter. The man on the phone said, "These are the kind of stories Mark loves to hear. I am going to see what I can do to arrange a meet and greet." My daughter and I were ushered from our seats and brought behind stage to meet him. I had brought a scrapbook with pictures of Jesse that Mark Shultz slowly looked through. The love of God was so evident in him. He hugged us tightly and introduced us to the members of the band Avalon who were also playing that night. It was such a blessing for us both.

> If you love me, keep my commands. And I will ask the Father, and he will give you another advocate to help you and be with you forever—the Spirit of truth. The world cannot accept him, because it neither sees him nor knows him. But you know him, for he lives with you and will be in you. I will not leave you as orphans; I will come to you. Before long, the world will not see me anymore, but you will see me. Because I live, you also will live. On that day you will realize that I am in my Father, and you are in me, and I am in you.
>
> —JOHN 14:15–20, NIV

> Keep your lives free from the love of money and be content with what you have, because God has said, "Never will I leave you; never will I forsake you."
>
> —HEBREWS 13:5, NIV

> *Thank you Lord for the free gift of salvation, that heaven is our true home, and that we have an eternity to spend with our loved ones that have gone before us in your name. Thank you for these*

dedicated, talented musicians who use their gifts
to bring you glory. In the name of Jesus, Amen.

SAMI AND MARK SCHULTZ AT HIS CONCERT

DREAMS FROM
THE LORD

As I enjoyed the peace and quiet of living on the plantation, it gave me much refuge to spend a lot of time outdoors creating my garden. My neighbor Jude who lived in the log cabin next door to me came over to the fence and welcomed me back. I reminded him that it had been five years since we first met when I bought the house. We could both hardly believe it. In reply to no matter what I said, he would respond, "Yes ma'am." I told him, "I understand that's the southern way, but it makes me feel old. I know, there's another southern greeting—*Darlin'*. You can call me that." We laughed.

To my surprise I never really felt afraid living alone, but I was glad to know he was within reach and had an arsenal of hunting rifles. We became quick friends. He gave me the key to his golf cart and sometimes I took it down to the beach two blocks away. I loved that beach on the St. Helena sound. I spent a lot of days there just sitting, praying, and writing. It was definitely a time of restoration as the Lord had told me it would be. There were horse stables on the other side of my house, and the horses passed by on their way to the beach. That was a constant reminder of the vision of the horse that God gave to Jesse. I spent many a day just thinking about what it must've been like for Adam and Eve in the garden. I knew this could not compare, yet it felt to me like I was in this place of beauty communing with the Lord.

Jude is a pastor's kid or as they say PK, and so I knew he knew the gospel and his big heart came through. He took me out on his boat one day with his cousin and wife. We had a great time just exploring the river. He told me about another island that they nicknamed Monkey Island because they did experiments on monkeys there. The only way to get to the island was by boat, and so he said we would go one day. Well, we never got to go, but I did go in a dream. It was my very first dream of Jesse, and it felt so real. In the dream we went to Monkey Island and Jesse was laughing hysterically. He was imitating the monkeys, scratching himself under his armpits and making their sounds as he watched them swinging from the trees.

He jumped off the side of the boat, swimming in the water just as he had always loved to do in our backyard pool and at the beach. I could almost touch the water in the dream and see how perfectly clear and blue it was. He was having such a good time. There are just certain dreams that I know in my heart and in my spirit are from the Lord. I knew He was letting me know that Jesse was laughing, and he was happy!

> He will wipe away every tear from their eyes, and death shall be no more, neither shall there be mourning, nor crying, nor pain anymore, for the former things have passed away.
>
> —REVELATION 21:4, ESV

Then the angel showed me the river of the water

of life, bright as crystal, flowing from the throne of God and of the Lamb through the middle of the street of the city; also, on either side of the river, the tree of life with its twelve kinds of fruit, yielding its fruit each month. The leaves of the tree were for the healing of the nations.

— REVELATION 22: 1–2, ESV

Therefore they are before the throne of God, and serve him day and night in his temple; and he who sits on the throne will shelter them with his presence. They shall hunger no more, neither thirst anymore; the sun shall not strike them, nor any scorching heat. For the Lamb in the midst of the throne will be their shepherd, and he will guide them to springs of living water, and God will wipe away every tear from their eyes.

— REVELATION 7:15–17, ESV

Lord,

Thank you that you give us pictures in your Word, in visions, and in dreams of our true home, heaven. I know that we cannot even begin to grasp the beauty that awaits us there. Thank you that we may be in the world but not of the world. We are citizens of heaven. Thank you for the beauty of your creation here on earth, a glimpse of what will be for us in heaven. In the name of Jesus, Amen.

THE CELEBRITY FILES

W hen Jesse got discouraged, the one thing that made him respond was music. When the music therapist came into the hospital room asking if she could play her guitar, no matter how he was feeling, he would always nod yes. Shortly after that he was given a bass guitar from his youth pastor when he heard that story. Jesse said to me, "Music is my life." We shared that passion. I wanted to learn the guitar, maybe more for him since he never got to. I didn't get too far, yet I'll never forget one early morning, I awoke hearing a song in my spirit that I knew I had never heard before. I got up to write the words that were coming to me as quickly as a computer can download a song. It was the Lord speaking to me!

In December 2001 the hospital gave a Christmas party at Sony Wonder on Madison Avenue. We had heard that Bruce Springsteen was going to be there, so I brought my "Born in the USA" album hoping to get his autograph. Jesse had no idea who he was and didn't want to stand in line to meet him. When I told Jesse that he played guitar, he thought that was cool and waited in line because he knew I was excited. Bruce Springsteen told me that he had a child named Jesse. Perhaps hearing Jesse's name really touched home for him.

His compassion was evident. The hospital said he came every year to this event. His manager joked with me asking me not to sell the album on eBay. My response was, "Let me see what the hospital bills are going to be first!"

Another fun outing was when we went to Planet Hollywood to see the premiere of the Ben Affleck and Jennifer Garner movie, "Daredevil." Jesse loved Jennifer and followed her all around that day. She was very popular from a TV show we watched together in the hospital called "Alias." She played a superwoman fighting crime. She signed a T-shirt for Jesse saying, "Maybe we can have a fight someday." It was so sweet watching him look at her. I felt so badly knowing he was forcing himself to have enough energy to enjoy the day. At one point he became so nauseous that he couldn't help but get sick in the room. Luckily the nurses were prepared, and it was somewhat discreet; however, I still remember Jennifer watching, and I saw the compassion on her face. The kids went in for the screening of the film while the parents had lunch with the stars. I couldn't help but notice Ben and Jennifer being a little cozier than just friends. Of course I went up to Ben later and said, "I thought you were engaged to JLo?"

"Oh yes, yes I am," he said. A few months later the papers wrote of their breakup, and the next thing you know he's marrying Jennifer! About a year later Jennifer came back to New York to film another movie. She saw the nurses and asked about Jesse. I was not surprised when they told me she remembered him.

Probably one of the most exciting times for Jesse was when Scott Niedermeyer of the New Jersey Devils brought the Stanley Cup to our house. Within a few minutes of his phone call, Jesse had all his friends over. It was quite the exciting evening. He had heard about Jesse when he purchased a vehicle from Jesse's dad. He also organized a fundraiser to help us pay some hospital bills.

I know the best time for Jesse had to be when he got to go into the Yankee dugout and meet the players. Joe Tori put the championship ring on his finger and Jason Giambi helped him learn how to pitch. He got to do the Verizon commercial on the teleprompter.

I think about how it is so easy in this world to strive, climb the corporate ladders, be competitive, become workaholics and maybe achieve success by how the world defines it—having money and fame. So many young people, especially young girls, are enamored by outward beauty and want to be like and look like models and movie stars. The stars we met appeared to understand that fame and beauty fade. They seemed to know that it could all be taken away in a moment. I believe that time helped to give my daughter the right perspective on the worldview of success and beauty. I could see that Sami was a nurturer from a young child playing with dolls. Now, having had a brother with cancer, seeing so many children suffer along with him, I believe helped to form her compassionate heart. It makes me so proud to see the woman she has become. Not only does she want to make her profession one that helps those that are less fortunate, she sees the inner beauty in everyone. This is yet another testament to how the Lord used this trial for good. I am also so proud of my son Matt who has become an independent, hard-working, dedicated man who serves our country in the military.

> Do not lay up for yourselves treasures on earth, where moth and rust destroy and where thieves break in and steal, but lay up for yourselves treasures in heaven, where neither moth nor rust destroys, and where thieves do not break in or steal. For where your treasure is, there your heart will be also.
>
> —MATTHEW 6:19–21, ESV

So we do not lose heart. Though our outer self is wasting away, our inner self is being renewed day by day.

—2 CORINTHIANS 4:16, ESV

Dear Lord,

Thank you for showing us that material things here on earth are worth nothing! Thank you for all you have given us to enjoy; may we always share what we have with others in need. Thank you for giving me a heart to realize what true treasures are: our righteousness because of Christ's righteousness and our inheritance as joint heirs to Christ Jesus. In the name of Jesus, Amen.

JESSE ENJOYING THE MUSIC THERAPIST AT THE HOSPITAL

JESSE AND BEN AFFLECK AT PLANET HOLLYWOOD

JESSE AND JENNIFER GARNER
SIGNING HIS SHIRT

JESSE AND SAMI WITH
JENNIFER LOVE-HEWITT AT
THE HOSPITAL

BRUCE SPRINGSTEEN AT SONY
WONDER CHRISTMAS PARTY

SAMI WITH MICHAEL J. FOX
AT SONY WONDER
CHRISTMAS PARTY

JASON GIAMBI AND JESSE

JESSE AND SAMI ENJOYING
A YANKEE GAME

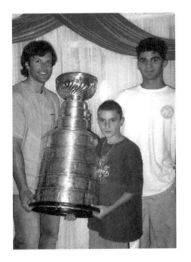

SCOTT NIEDERMAYER
WITH JESSE AND MATT IN
OUR LIVING ROOM HOLDING
THE STANLEY CUP

PASTOR TIM

I had been feeling weary during the process of writing these stories down on paper. Not that I ever will or want to forget any of the people or circumstances surrounding the journey with Jesse, but it can be difficult recalling hard times. My life with my husband now is filled with such joy and laughter, and most days I'd like to just stay in that place, yet I know that is not how the Lord is using us for His glory. He's proven over and over to us that when we give of ourselves to others—reveal the lessons learned and give testimony of God's faithfulness from our painful trials—more healing takes place for us and blessings begin to flow.

One morning I was finding it so hard to sit and listen or write. I told God that He really needed to intervene (as if He doesn't always need to) because I was feeling dry. I know we have dry seasons sometimes, and we can't always be on the mountaintop in our spiritual walk. The waiting and wanting to have that renewed sense of passion again was really getting to me. I admit that I don't much like to wait for anything. I knew God would come through, and oh, how He did that day. I decided to rid myself of my many distractions first by searching on the web for a non-denominational church near the town my husband and I were looking to move to. When the church name came up, I didn't read about the pastor or anything else, I just clicked on the latest sermon to listen to it. It was appropriately titled, "Heaven is for Real." As I listened, the Holy Spirit came over me with new revelation of the scriptures I had heard before, such as, "He will wipe every tear from their eyes, and there will be no more death or sorrow or crying or pain. All these things are gone forever" (Revelation 21:4, NLT). I just began to weep in the truth of this hope that we have.

I began to praise God and felt renewed in my spirit. The rest of the day I could not shake the thought of calling the church. I argued with myself how stupid that would be. I did have thoughts and questions I would have liked to ask the pastor, but I reasoned to myself that I was a stranger to the church; I couldn't just call. I finally relented telling myself that the secretary would just tell me he's not available and would I like his voicemail or email. Suddenly I knew that the sense to call was from the Lord when the pastor immediately got on the phone. I told him a little bit about that morning, my writing the story about what God had done since my son went home to be with Him, and there was complete silence for a moment until I could hear the pastor's voice begin to quiver as he said, "My son just passed away six months ago!" It was such a divine appointment. Sometimes in life there is no better way to encourage others that to just say, "Me too." We talked for almost an hour. He shared his heartache and loss, knowing I understood his pain. He talked about Jacob who wrestled with God in Genesis chapter 32, and how we might be struggling with God about the passing of our sons way too soon. This story shows us that the struggle is exhausting. It could leave us crippled if we don't come to grips with God and know we can't go on without Him. For when Jacob finally surrendered, he received God's blessing. He chose Jacob to be the father of the nation of Israel although he was not a "good" man. Jacob did something brave. He refused to give up until God blessed him. He continued to fight, but now *for* God, not against Him! We agreed that this is what we both needed to choose also. I think we reminded each other that day of a lesson in humility as well as the promises of God for us. In the Bible we see time and time again that people who accomplished amazing things for God had experienced great pain. Pastor Tim said, "We may always, on this side of heaven, walk *with a limp* like Jacob, but we have been *marked* by God with authority." God is all-powerful and worthy of all our praise! With that heart attitude, we can't lose. There's not a story in the Bible that isn't there for each one of us. There's another, perhaps corny, acronym I like for BIBLE: Book of Information Before we Leave Earth! How foolish not to read our directions more carefully. He goes before us and leads us along straight paths, never leaving us! We need not fear.

The pastor also reminded me of the following scripture:

> Therefore; since we are surrounded by such a great cloud of witnesses, let us throw off everything that hinders and the sin that so easily entangles. And let us run with perseverance the race marked out for us, fixing our eyes on Jesus, the pioneer and perfecter of faith. For the joy set before him he endured the cross, scorning its shame, and sat down at the right hand of the throne of God.
>
> —HEBREWS 12:1–2, NIV

Yes, it is a race we need to endure; yet we already know that we have won the race! The victory is ours in Christ.

Did I mention that the church was two hours north from the

town that I had Google searched!

Lord,

Thank you that Jesse's life encouraged me to live mine in faith. Thank you for giving me a picture of Jesse and you cheering me on to run the race with the same victory Jesse has obtained, that by your faithfulness I will not be overwhelmed! I pray that as people see my "limp" they will see you and know it is for your glory, made by your loving hands. In the name of Jesus, Amen.

MARC AND CHERYL

I was reliving in my mind the night Chip asked me to marry him. He jokes now that at the time, he argued with the Lord that he couldn't ask me to marry him yet because he didn't have a ring. He felt that was just not the way it was supposed to be done. Even though on many levels it was out of his comfort zone, the Lord spoke to him, and he obeyed. His obedience to the Lord is just one more thing I love about him. He called his brother-in-law Marc after hearing from the Lord so clearly that day he prayed about us on the beach. Marc has always had great Godly wisdom to share and was not surprised that God was blessing Chip for his perseverance and faithfulness. Cheryl and Chip are very close in age, and they grew up doing everything together from going door-to-door selling candy to raise money for their school to getting into trouble together for cutting school. Marc and Cheryl have always been a vital support for Chip throughout the sickness and loss of his wife of nearly thirty years. Marc went through a dramatic conversion from being a Christian to being of "follower of Jesus" and ultimately becoming a pastor. When he announced he was quitting his job to go to Bible College one Thanksgiving dinner, Chip tells the story that he warned Marc he shouldn't joke like that, especially in front of the family. They have shared life together for a long time and their selfless love and commitment for one another runs very deep. Marc and Cheryl were at Chip's side during the horrific times of his wife's illness, and they continued to pray for Chip through his years of grief. They constantly prayed that his faith would remain strong in the Lord as so many of us get angry when God doesn't answer our prayers the way we had hoped. For the next six years alone, Chip drenched himself in God's Word and grew even closer to the Lord. He gained strength from God's Word and persevered. He recalled the day he came home from church and just fell to his knees asking God for a change in his life. God was leading Chip into a happy, fulfilled life again and although he didn't know what that would look like, he listened, trusted, and obeyed. Shortly after that prayer he started to drive seven hundred miles to see me in South Carolina, having been just email friends for two years! He thought it would just be a fun trip, and that I would be his personal tour guide. I knew already that it would be more than that! Marc and Cheryl were thrilled for us as they praised God for answered prayers and for His great redemption in both our lives. It was such an honor to have Marc marry us, knowing how Chip felt about his "twin brother" who was born the same day and year as him! We were so thrilled to have him be part of our special day. I started to pray for our future, and I felt the Lord direct me to a painting given to me by my friend Lisa. On it was this scripture: "…No eye has seen, no ear has heard, no mind has imagined what God has prepared for those who love him" (1 Corinthians 2:9, NLT). I knew this was what the Lord was telling me. His promises are so true! This would be our marriage verse.

I shared that testimony with Marc and Cheryl when we met with them to go over the wedding ceremony. Marc and Cheryl presented us with such a treasured wedding gift: a wood plaque with that scripture from 1 Corinthians. They also thoughtfully had vines and leaves engraved on it as I spoke about another verse from God's Word: "I am the vine; you are the branches. If you remain in me and I in you, you will bear much fruit; apart from me you can do nothing" (John 15:5, NIV).

I am so honored and grateful to have Marc and Cheryl as my new family. God has truly increased my life with such loving, caring individuals. Very recently my husband and I had the opportunity to visit Marc and Cheryl in their home. What a blessed time we had of just talking, laughing, and praying together. We discovered that they lived only a few miles from a village called "Give Kids the World," a place I had come with Jesse. The village hosts families with children having life-threatening illnesses and shuttles them to Disney. Marc informed us that many of the members of his church volunteer there often. We went there to see Jesse's star as they placed one for each visiting child. We also found the paver stone that we had inscribed nearly fourteen years ago.

Going there that day reminded me of the "Sacred Ripples" that sometimes intersect. It was an honor and a privilege to share that place, those memories, with family who had never met Jesse, yet love the story God wrote for him.

> Do nothing from selfish ambition or conceit, but in humility count others more significant than yourselves. Let each of you look not only to his own interests, but also to the interests of others. Have this mind among yourselves, which is yours in Christ Jesus, who, though he was in the form of God, did not count equality with God a thing to be grasped, but emptied himself, by taking the form of a servant, being born in the likeness of men.
>
> —PHILIPPIANS 2:3–7, ESV

Thank you Lord for the gift of family, for Marc and Cheryl, and for his willingness and obedience to follow the call you had on his life to be a pastor. Thank you for their fervent constant prayers. We ask, Holy Spirit, that you continue to pour into Marc and Cheryl, your faithful servants. Thank you, Lord, for the privilege of lifting each other up to your throne in prayer. May we be faithful in our prayers for each other as you are faithful. In the name of Jesus, Amen.

CONCLUSION

I realize that I used the word *redeeming* quite often in my stories. I did that primarily because I believe that it accurately sums up the result of all God does for those who obey His first and greatest commandment: to love Him with all your heart, and with all your soul, and all your mind. He will then strengthen us to hold on to *hope*, keep *faith* alive, *trust* Him, and wait on Him as we passionately seek to know Him more!

Redemption in Scripture is that God has taken the initiative to act compassionately for all of us who are powerless to help ourselves. Please, please don't let guilt and shame keep you from moving forward in your walk with the Lord! It's a process—we are all being sanctified (made holy) and His mercies are new every day.

"The steadfast love of the LORD NEVER CEASES; HIS MERCIES NEVER COME TO AN END; they are new every morning; great is your faithfulness" (Lamentations 3:22–23, ESV).

As humans we tend to use *coping mechanisms* to ease our pain. Trust me, they don't work for long. It's also not about *behavior modification*. We cannot change ourselves—only He can do it for us, and He wants to! Why not just surrender your trying to Him? The word *surrender* makes us think of giving up, but in the eyes of Lord, it's giving back our lives to Him—the One who created us so that He can be the Perfect Potter and mold us, remake us to the image of His perfect Son. "And yet, O LORD, you are our Father. We are the clay, and you are the potter. We all are formed by your hand" (Isaiah 64:8, NLT).

By sending His Son as the final sacrifice, a ransom for all our sins, the price has been paid so that it costs us nothing! Jesus paid the price! Salvation is a free gift for those who want to receive it. This knowledge can be just in our minds, or we can experience it in our hearts by believing His Word is true and relevant for our lives. It is *transforming*, and it is *redeeming*! He wants to keep hope alive and give you unshakable joy!

"And so, LORD, where do I put my hope? My only hope is in you" (Psalms 39:7, NLT).

"For you know that God paid a ransom to save you from the empty life you inherited from your ancestors. And it was not paid with mere gold or silver, which lose their value. It was the precious blood of Christ, the sinless, spotless Lamb of God" (1 Peter 1:18–19, NLT).

Thank you for taking the time to read these stories and for allowing me to share just a part of what God has done for Chip and me. We pray that you would know that He wants to do the same for you!

If this is your heart desire, just pray a simple prayer admitting that you are a sinner and you are sorry for your sins; invite Jesus into your heart as your Savior, and believe in your heart that His Word is true—that He died for your sins and rose from the dead! Commit your new life to Him and the promise of heaven is yours.

If you prayed that prayer the angels are rejoicing in heaven because eternity is now yours! Read His Word, pray back His Word to Him, and remember the prayer that Jesus Himself gave to us to pray:

> *Our Father in heaven, may your name be kept holy.*
> *May your Kingdom come soon. May your will be*
> *done on earth, as it is in heaven. Give us today the*
> *food we need, and forgive us our sins, as we have*
> *forgiven those who sin against us. And don't let us*
> *yield to temptation, but rescue us from the evil one.*
> *[For yours is the kingdom and the power and the*
> *glory forever and ever. Amen.]*
>
> —MATTHEW 6:9–13, NLT

ABOUT THE AUTHOR

Marian Newell, together with the support of her husband and family, continues "Jesse's Wish"—a 501 3(c) nonprofit foundation.

"Jesse's Wish" was started by Jesse himself to help find a bone marrow match for his friend at the hospital. Jesse's legacy has expanded and through the proceeds of *The Sacred Ripple* will continue to help families with children suffering through cancer treatment.

Please visit thesacredripple.com for more information or email Marian at contact@thesacredripple.com